Prun 90

D1429570

# TORY & WHIG

*The Struggle in the Constituencies 1701–1715*

# Tory & Whig

## *The Struggle in the Constituencies*
## 1701–1715

W. A. SPECK

Macmillan
St Martin's Press

*First published* 1970 *by*
MACMILLAN AND CO LTD
*Little Essex Street London* WC2
*and also at Bombay Calcutta and Madras*
*Macmillan South Africa (Publishers) Pty Ltd Johannesburg*
*The Macmillan Company of Australia Pty Ltd Melbourne*
*The Macmillan Company of Canada Ltd Toronto*
*St Martin's Press Inc New York*
*Gill and Macmillan Ltd Dublin*

*Library of Congress catalog card no.* 73–97057

*Printed in Great Britain by*
RICHARD CLAY (THE CHAUCER PRESS) LTD
*Bungay, Suffolk*

*for*

SHEILA

# Contents

# Preface

WHILE writing this book I have incurred heavy debts of obligation to a great many people. When I was searching for materials I came to appreciate the acknowledgements paid by other historians to the courtesy and help which they had received in those familiar institutions, the Bodleian Library and the British Museum. In addition I obtained invaluable assistance from the Royal Historical Manuscripts Commission and the National Register of Archives. In their offices I was introduced to the existence of less familiar materials in private hands, public libraries and local record offices throughout England and Wales.

This information took me to the private archives of the duke of Marlborough at Blenheim, the duke of Northumberland at Alnwick, the marquess of Bath at Longleat, the earl of Bradford at Weston Park, Lord Hampton at the Old Rectory, Holt, Lord Methuen at Corsham Court, and Sir Richard and Lady Hamilton at Walton Hall. I also visited the late Admiral the Honourable Sir Reginald Plunkett-Ernle-Erle-Drax at Charborough Park, whose papers were subsequently deposited in Churchill College, Cambridge, and consulted at Studley Royal the papers of the late Commander C. G. Vynen, which have since been transferred to the West Riding Record Office in Leeds. Finally I wish to reserve a special note of thanks for Mrs O. R. Bagot's splendid hospitality on my visits to Levens Hall.

I wrote to and visited too many libraries and record offices to mention them all here – those which yielded relevant materials are listed in the Bibliography. But I should like to thank all the librarians and archivists who so patiently and helpfully answered my inquiries, and particularly Mr B. C. Jones and Miss Sheila Macpherson of the

Cumberland and Westmorland Joint Archives Committee, who went well beyond the normal course of professional duty to assist my researches. I am grateful, too, to the owners of papers deposited in libraries and record offices for allowing historians to quote from them. The duke of Portland is an especial benefactor of those working in this period for giving them access to his vast manuscript collection in the libraries of the British Museum and Nottingham University. This particular study also drew extensively on the manuscripts of the earl of Lonsdale, Lord Egremont and Sir Gyles Isham, Bt.

To gain access to the materials on which this study is based required financial assistance, which I obtained from various sources. Without the travel allowances paid by the Ministry of Education between 1960 and 1962, when I was a State Student, and by the University of Exeter from 1962 to 1963, when I was a tutor there, I could never have afforded to visit so many repositories in those years on my own slender resources. The University of Newcastle upon Tyne, which I joined in 1963, has been extremely generous to me, particularly in the purchase of microfilm copies of documents. In 1967 I benefited considerably from the generosity of the Huntington Library and the Twenty Seven Foundation, which financed a visit to San Marino, where so much material bearing on early-eighteenth-century Britain lies almost undisturbed in late-twentieth-century California. I am grateful to all these owners for permitting me to use their family papers. I am grateful to the Director of the Huntington Library for permitting me to publish a document in the Ellesmere manuscripts as an appendix.

One of the greatest pleasures of research is to exchange ideas and information with other historians working in the same field. I have gained a great deal from conversations and correspondence with Dr J. Cannon of Bristol University, Dr H. T. Dickinson of Edinburgh University, Dr E. Ellis of the University of Wales, and Dr H. L. Snyder of Kansas University. This book is based on part of my Oxford D.Phil. thesis, which owed much to the suggestions of my fellow-student Dr H. Horwitz, now of Iowa University, and of our supervisor, the Rev. Dr G. V. Bennett of New College, Oxford. More recent versions of it have gained from the criticisms of Professor J. H. Plumb of Christ's College, Cambridge. At every stage it has benefited beyond measure from the advice and example of Mr Geoffrey Holmes of Glasgow University, *il miglior fabbro.* The faults of this final version, however, are all my own work.

*Newcastle upon Tyne*                                      W. A. S.
*October 1968*

# Note on Dates

Throughout this book all dates are given in the Old Style, though the year is taken to have begun on 1 January.

There were two General Elections in 1701, one in January, the other in December. The starting-point of this study is the second of these elections, and unless January is specifically mentioned, some such expression as 'the 1701 election' refers to the General Election held in December.

# CHAPTER ONE

# Introduction

> *He wished he could have spared the invidious names of Whig
> and Tory, High and Low church, and other discriminating
> appellations: But since the Best and the Politest in their
> Discourses and writings are forced to use them, to avoid tedious
> circumlocutions, he hopes their Example will bear him out.*
>
> ABEL BOYER, *The Political State of
> Great Britain for* 1711

THE study of late Stuart politics has recently been rerouted from the
sidings into which it had been shunted since the Second World War
back onto the main line of historical investigation.[1] It is now no
longer open to doubt that the politics of the period were moulded by
a major contest between two parties, the Tories and the Whigs.
These parties were divided primarily over great issues concerning the
nature of government, the religious settlement and the objects of
foreign policy. Thus the Tories continued to prefer divine right
theories of government, were uneasy first about the Revolution
Settlement and then, at the prospect of the Hanoverian succession,
wished to protect such privileges of the Church of England as its
statutory monopoly of local and national offices, and disliked the deep
involvement in European affairs which was the consequence of
William III's accession. The Whigs, on the other hand, advocated
contractual kingship, ardently supported both the Revolution and the
Protestant succession, were anxious to defend dissenters against the
arbitrary exercise of its legal power by the Anglican Church, and
backed with increasing conviction England's commitment as a major
power to the system of alliances built up in Europe to contain
Louis XIV.

These issues were fundamental to post-Revolution politics. But where it seemed that they had been put on ice in 1689, they flared up again at the outset of the eighteenth century and dominated the party struggle between 1701 and 1715.

In the last year of William's reign they assumed fresh importance and thereby intensified the party struggle. The succession problem, apparently solved by the Bill of Rights in 1689, was reopened when the death of Anne's only child to survive babyhood occurred in 1700. The Act of Settlement of 1701 placed the succession in the House of Hanover, but the misgivings of many Tories on that occasion were obvious. Their doubts were further highlighted by their reluctance to subscribe to the oath laid down in the last Act to receive William's assent, whereby M.P.s, clergymen and office-holders had to abjure any allegiance to the Pretender. The religious question had ostensibly been settled by the Toleration Act of 1689, but the situation was disturbed by the increasing number of dissenters who occasionally took communion in the Anglican Church in order to qualify for office, and by the flood of anti-clerical literature released on the expiry of the Licensing Act in 1695. These trends alarmed the Anglican clergy, who raised the cry 'the Church in danger'. The Tories sought through Parliament and Convocation to suppress both abuses. Convocation met for the first time in over a decade in 1701; in 1702 a Bill was first introduced into Parliament to stamp out the practice of occasional conformity. Finally in 1701 the prospect of war with France again became imminent. The Whigs wanted to unite the country behind the Grand Alliance, which William was constructing to meet the threat from Louis XIV. Meanwhile the Tories displayed a marked reluctance to renew hostilities and an enthusiasm for finding scapegoats for the deteriorating international situation which led to the impeachment of four Whig peers.

The coincidence of these events in 1701–2 moulded the party struggle into a shape which was not drastically altered until after the Hanoverian succession. Another pattern emerged only when the Tory party could no longer offer a valid alternative to Whig rule, when the Whig party had itself fallen asunder, and when the great issues which had given the contest its dynamic disappeared. The question of war with France was concluded with the treaty of Utrecht in 1713; the succession problem was finally solved with the failure of the 'Fifteen; and the religious disputes were resolved with the demise of Convocation in 1717 and the repeal of the Occasional Conformity and Schism Acts in 1719.

If so much is clear about the ideological nature of the struggle, it has also been established that it extended far beyond the confines of Parliament. It involved not merely the classes which provided the membership of the two Houses, but comprehended the electorate and even to some extent the unenfranchised.

The House of Commons reflected the political predominance of a narrow social *élite*. Whereas during the Interregnum England had been governed at one time by major-generals of very humble social origins – butchers' sons, thimble-makers, sellers of leather points – under the later Stuarts the old social hierarchy reasserted itself. The Restoration was as much a restoration of the country's traditional ruling classes as of the king. Not the least important precipitant of the Revolution of 1688 was the attempt by James II to interfere with their privileges. In reaction to the extremists who had threatened the whole social order, whether from below or above, those who, in the contemporary phrase, had a 'permanent fixed interest' in the country combined to create, in the Revolution Settlement, government of the property-owners, for the property-owners, by the property-owners.

In the late seventeenth century power was vested in property and wealth, and above all, since England was still overwhelmingly rural, in landed property, though the accumulation of capital in London had made the City almost a separate estate of the realm. It was not until the nineteenth century was well under way that this equilibrium was disturbed by the next seismic shock to the social system, the Industrial Revolution. Until then the country was ruled mainly by its substantial landowners, its wealthiest businessmen and its leading professional men. Throughout the period 1701–15 the Members of the House of Commons were drawn almost exclusively from a social range which spanned at most 0·5 per cent of the total population.

That representatives should be selected from this narrow circle was regarded by its members as being part of the natural order of things. Lord Ashburnham was most indignant when a tradesman had the impertinence to upset it by standing against his son as a

parliamentary candidate at Hastings in November 1701. He wrote
to his son's running partner a letter brimming with aristocratic
spleen:[2]

> my son seems at present to have only a stranger tradesman for his
> competitor, and I flatter myself, hoping you will forgive a father's
> weakness, that my son is an honest Englishman and will acquit
> himself faithfully in his duty to his King and Country. As for his
> abilities, those few the times have allowed him an opportunity to
> acquire will be improved, I hope daily, by the good company of
> the gentlemen of the House of Commons. And for other circum-
> stances, he has such a stake in our English Hedge as may serve
> for a security for his integrity and good behaviour there. . . . As
> for the tradesman in question, whose name nor trade I do not
> rightly remember, who stands as they say at Hastings, I conceive
> such a person can never be approved nor admitted to pass in line
> of account with you and my son. . . .

Ashburnham was scandalised when his son was beaten at the polls
That the rights of property should be so rudely disregarded was too
much for him. 'My son has had the misfortune at Hastings to have
bribery used against him by one John Mouncher, ropemaker of
Portsmouth,' he exploded, 'a fellow that I believe such an one has
not sat in the House of Commons since the Conquest, and that's a
bold word.'[3]

Though Lord Ashburnham was a Tory, his belief in the rights of
landed property was not peculiar to that party. It was shared, for
instance, by James Lowther, a staunch Whig, who complained in
1708, 'there never was more need of men of estates to be chosen, when
officers of the army and merchants of London are jostling the landed
men everywhere out of their elections'.[4] Landowners of both parties
welcomed the Act of 1711 which restricted membership of Parliament
more closely to the landed classes by obliging M.P.s to possess real
estate worth £600 per annum for knights of the shire and £300 for
borough Members. When it was passed, it was a Whig who commented approvingly, 'every merchant, banker, or other monied man,
who is ambitious of serving his country as a senator, should have also
a competent, visible land estate, as a pledge to his electors that he
intends to abide by them'.[5]

Such views were, however, far more commonly expressed in Tory circles. Though it was a contemporary commonplace that Parliament should represent those with a permanent fixed interest in the country, the Tories were inclined to assert that this gave landowners a superior stake in the commonwealth, since land was more permanent and fixed than any other form of wealth, and particularly monied wealth. They therefore identified the landed interest with the national interest – Francis Atterbury called it 'the political blood of the nation'.[6] Tory assumptions that they represented the national interest while the Whigs reflected narrower, sectional interests convinced them that they had a greater right to rule. These convictions were beautifully illustrated in a pamphlet put out by the Tories during the Leicestershire election of 1715:[7]

> the honest Gentlemen here [the Tories] did once more design to be represented in the ensuing House of Commons by those two worthy Baronets Sir Jeffrey Palmer and Sir Thomas Cave, and all things went fairly on to their being chosen without any trouble or opposition, when on a sudden the Faction [the Whigs] at a joint charge set up a mushroom gentleman as a candidate of their own. . . .
>
> If he quarrels with me for the name of mushroom gentleman, I believe upon a little reflection all the world will vindicate me in using the word. For I must inform you, he is but the second generation of what sprouted from the dunghill, and just come from being a linen-draper behind the counter. As to his wits and estate, it is much to be feared he will never come to them at all; for all the wit the family ever had, lies buried in the grave with his father; and his estate is in as strict durance by mortgages, as parchment, ink and wax can make it. . . .

It was no accident, then, that the Property Qualifications Act was passed when the Tories had a large majority in the House of Commons. On the whole the landed credentials of Tory Members were more substantial than those of the Whigs. In any House of Commons the bulk of the Tory side consisted of country gentlemen, while the Whig party contained a greater proportion of merchants, lawyers, army officers and other professional men.

Nevertheless M.P.s of both persuasions were generally men of substance, even before the Property Qualifications Bill became law.

Looking back from the more egalitarian society of the twentieth
century to the House of Commons of the early eighteenth, one is
struck by the social cohesion of the political nation. Relatively few
in numbers, socially, economically and politically distinct from the
mass of the population below them, bound together by innumerable
family ties, the men who wielded real power in England then, those
who virtually monopolised its parliamentary representation, seem to
have formed one united class with a permanent fixed interest in the
preservation of the *status quo*.

Had this in fact been so, there need have been no struggle in the
constituencies between 1701 and 1715. But the seeming harmony
of interests among the members of the governing class is deceptive.
In reality they were bitterly divided. Between the component sections
of the political nation – the landed interest, the monied interest,
merchants, professional and military men – there was increasing
friction as the long wars against Louis XIV put a disproportionate
fiscal burden on the mere landowners, and to some extent benefited
the other interests. This created a clash of interests which exacerbated
the already fierce ideological conflict that divided the ruling *élite*.[8]
Unable to agree among themselves, they competed for the support of
the electorate below them.

In Northamptonshire, for example, real political influence was
limited to a handful of prominent families – the Berties, Cartwrights,
Cecils, Dudleys, Finches, Hattons, Ishams, Montagues and Spencers.
If they had been able to pool their interests behind the same candidates,
the freeholders of that county would never have had the chance to
exercise their right to vote. But their differences were such that they
were unable to accommodate them, and they split into two parties
which fielded rival candidates at three general elections between 1701
and 1715. There were no local reasons why their disputes should
divide them into two camps, nor anything to stop them from forming
any number of possible combinations. Indeed for much of William's
reign Northamptonshire politics were marked by the formation of
unstable shifting alliances between the various families. In 1701,
however, 'there stood opposite each other two interests which can
for the first time be considered with some certainty as the beginning
of the conflicting Tory and Whig interests in the county for the

succeeding period – the Whig interest centring in Sunderland, and that of the Tories in the friends of Sir Justinian Isham backed by a variety of aristocratic connections'.[9]

This polarisation of interests in Northamptonshire coincided with the intensification of the party struggle in the last year of William's reign. From then until 1715 the parties were polarised not only in Parliament but throughout the constituencies into what contemporaries termed the 'Church' or 'Tory interest', and the 'Whig interest'. When Henry St John was invited to stand in Berkshire he resolved 'to neglect nothing in my power which may contribute towards making the Church interest the prevailing one in our county', while James Butler, on being sounded as to his willingness to contest Sussex, replied that he would 'if it be for the Whig interest'.[10] Writing to the earl of Sunderland about plans for a contest in Coventry in 1705, George Lucy informed him of a proposal 'made in writing and signed by betwixt 20 and 30 of the chief of the Whig interest'.[11] Of his candidature at Cricklade in 1708 James Vernon noted 'that vacancy was made for me by the death of Mr Barker of Fairford, and I stood upon his interest which was the Whig interest. . . . I was opposed by Mr Godard, a Wiltshire gentleman, upon the Tory interest.'[12]

Between 1701 and 1715 most contested elections took the form of straight party fights. In theory any number of candidates could stand for election in any constituency. Yet in London most general elections saw four Tories and four Whigs fighting for the capital's 4 seats. Apart from Weymouth, which like London returned four Members, and five boroughs which were represented by one M.P. apiece, the English constituencies each had 2 seats in Parliament.

In the typical two-Member constituency of the early eighteenth century a contest produced three or four candidates, with both parties either fielding two apiece, or one putting up a single candidate against partners provided by the other side. This pattern was sometimes disturbed, as in Yorkshire where five candidates stood in 1708. But even there it is obvious from the votes cast that the electorate regarded only four of them as serious contenders and the other as an outsider.[13] Occasionally, too, candidates of the same party would make interest on their own behalf, as in Nottinghamshire in 1710 where it was reported that two Tories and two Whigs stood 'all on their own legs'.[14] It was very rare, however, for members of the same party to oppose each other. The Tory interest in Devon split on one occasion, at a by-election held in 1712, where one group of Tories supported Sir William Courtenay while another backed Sir William Pole.[15] When a similar situation threatened in Leicestershire in 1711, Sir Justinian Isham was 'not a little concerned that two Gentlemen both of the same principles should oppose one another', and one of the candidates confessed 'I would be unhappy to have the Church interest once divided'.[16] The Tory interest became so divided nationally in 1713 that at some contests in the General Election of that year Hanoverian Tories fought Jacobites. There was no exact parallel for this on the Whig side, and indeed any cases of internal strife among the Whigs were very unusual in the constituencies as in Parliament. They were exceptional enough even among the Tories when contrasted with the great number of occasions when the men who wielded electoral influence combined to form Tory and Whig interests which held together through seven general elections between 1701 and 1715.

This unique run of elections came to an end when the Septennial Act become law in 1716. The change from triennial elections was bound to affect the pattern of politics in the constituencies regardless of any other considerations, for it meant that the heated, feverish atmosphere of almost permanent electioneering would cool down, making for greater stability. Its impact was even more decisive, however, because it coincided with the radical change in the context of national politics which followed the death of Queen Anne. When the next General Election was held in 1722, therefore, the nature of political conflict in the constituencies, as in the country, was very greatly altered. The struggle between Tory and Whig had been decided.

It will be obvious from what has already been stated that some knowledge of the nature of the unreformed electoral system is basic to an appreciation of the struggle in the constituencies during this period. Those who are familiar with the outstanding features of that system can skip the rest of this Introduction. Since the argument in the following chapters assumes such knowledge, however, others might prefer to be introduced beforehand to some of the terms which are employed in them to describe the workings of the eighteenth-century electoral machinery.

Throughout this book constituencies are classified according to a convention generally adopted by historians. This categorises them first by the type of franchise prevailing within them, and secondly by the size of their electorates.

Before 1832 there were basically five voting qualifications in England and Wales. Scotland presents its own constitutional and political peculiarities, and although it sent forty-five Members to the Parliament of Great Britain after 1707, it has been left outside the scope of this study. In the fifty-two counties the franchise was fixed in the ownership of freeholds valued at forty shillings per annum. That obtaining in the parliamentary boroughs, however, was very far from being uniform. In some the right to vote went with the possession of pieces of real estate known as burgages, or even 'votable burgages'. These could vary from a respectable field to a dilapidated barn. In some places the tenants of these properties voted, while in others the proprietors exercised the right.

In other towns the right to vote was restricted to the members of the corporation. A typical eighteenth-century town council consisted of a mayor, twelve aldermen and twenty-four common council men. There were nineteen boroughs in which such officials alone could vote. In many more boroughs, on the other hand, the franchise was enjoyed by the freemen. The status of freemen could be acquired through inheritance, by membership of a company or from the corporation.

Another form of qualification was residential. At Preston this meant nothing more – or less – than overnight residence before an election. Elsewhere, however, restrictions operated. In many boroughs inhabitant householders not in receipt of alms or charity were enfranchised. Since these could fend for themselves, and could therefore boil their own pot, they were known as potwallers or potwallopers. In some towns the vote was even more restricted, being confined to those householders who paid local rates.

These categories cover all the franchise qualifications in English and Welsh constituencies during this period, except that which operated in the universities of Oxford and Cambridge. In these, those who obtained the degree of M.A. thereby acquired the right to vote. There were towns where the categories were mixed. For example, in Hertford the electorate was divided almost evenly between inhabitants and freemen; of the 537 who voted there in 1705 282 fell into the first category and most of the rest into the second.[17] Nevertheless the prevalent franchise can readily be ascertained in most cases. Enough, at least, to classify forty-one constituencies as burgage boroughs, nineteen as corporation boroughs, one hundred as freemen boroughs and fifty-five as inhabitant boroughs.

While the prevalent franchise is a useful pointer to the political situation within a constituency, the size of the electorate is often a more significant indication. Discrepancies in the size of the electorate from constituency to constituency were even more marked, ranging from the 9000 or so voters of Yorkshire to ten or twelve in Old Sarum. Contemporaries recognised this in the etiquette of preference given to different constituencies. Counties were regarded as the cream of the Constitution. If a candidate was chosen in two places, one of which was a county and the other a borough, he was in honour bound to accept the county seat. There were exceptions to this rule 'It is esteemed as great an honour to be one of the representatives of the City of London as it is to be chosen a knight of a shire for any county whatsoever,'[18] observed one contemporary, while the dons of Oxford thought poorly of Sir Christopher Musgrave for stepping down from representing the university in order to sit as Member for Westmorland.[19] By and large, however, the pyramid of honours was tacitly understood in this as in other aspects of life in this period. Today we prefer broad categorisation rather than finely graded hierarchies, and it simplifies the electoral structure if the 269 constituencies are divided into large, medium and small, with the 96 having over 500 voters in the first group, the 98 with between 100 and 500 in the second, and the 75 with under 100 in the third.

Another term frequently encountered in the pages that follow is 'interest', though this was used by contemporaries and has not been coined by modern historians. The concept of interest was extremely elastic, and stretched far beyond the sphere of parliamentary elections.

In that context, however, to have an interest meant being able to exert some influence in a constituency, from simply having the right to vote there, to owning sufficient property, in a burgage borough for example, to be able to nominate both Members.

These features of the electoral system were constant factors from the enfranchisement of Newark, the last borough to become a parliamentary constituency by royal fiat, in 1673, to the disfranchisement of Grampound in 1821. But, as this book seeks to demonstrate, the period 1701 to 1715 was in many respects a distinct epoch within the era which opens with the Restoration of Charles II and closes with the passing of the first Reform Act in 1832. Among the distinctive features of that epoch which it might be as well to delineate at the outset were the key individuals who dominated the electoral scene.

On the Whig side far and away the biggest electoral manager of the period was undoubtedly Lord Wharton, who assisted the elections of Whig candidates in Cumberland and Westmorland in the North-West, Yorkshire in the North, Northamptonshire in the Midlands, Buckinghamshire and Oxfordshire in the South, and Wiltshire in the West. The duke of Newcastle, who was the uncle of the more famous duke of Walpole's day, had interests in almost as many constituencies as Wharton, but most of these were concentrated in Yorkshire and Nottinghamshire. The duke of Somerset had fewer interests to manage, but if anything these were more scattered geographically, from Northumberland and Cumberland to Sussex and Wiltshire.

On the Tory side there was no electoral magnate to rival Wharton, though the duke of Beaufort could hold his own with the other leading Whig peers, cultivating interests in numerous constituencies from Monmouthshire and South Wales across Gloucestershire and down into Hampshire. For the first half of the period, until his death in 1708, Sir Edward Seymour was the head of a formidable Tory interest in the West Country, which Defoe once called 'Seymskeyes Western Empire'.[20]

To these kings of the electoral system could be added dozens of princes who managed their party's affairs in more restricted spheres. Thus the Whigs of Norfolk were headed by the young Robert

Walpole and his friend Lord Townshend, while those of Dorset and
Wiltshire were led by the duke of Bolton and the third earl of
Shaftesbury. Among the more energetic Tory managers was Sir
Charles Shuckburgh, who was the key link in a chain of influence
which joined together Tory interests in Gloucestershire, Northampton-
shire and Warwickshire.

These chains of influence bound together Tory and Whig electoral
interests throughout England and Wales. It was not until the Tory
party ceased to command a national following and the Whig party
disintegrated into rival factions that the links joining the component
interests were shattered. Where later the electoral map came to
resemble a patchwork of warring interests, in the years 1701 to 1715,
whatever shades are used to depict various constituent parts, it can
be painted in two colours, one for the Tories and the other for the
Whigs.

# CHAPTER TWO

# The Electorate

*I am very sensible that were it not for so great and good an end as the Honour and Interest of our Country, very few men of honest principles would engage themselves with such sort of people as are electors in some places, not to say in most places of England. I should be much concerned if the majority of the House should resemble the majority of the electors in any Parliament.*

LORD ASHBURNHAM to MARTIN FOLKES,
26 Nov 1701

MODERN psephologists can fairly readily reconstruct the size and shape of the electorate for any period since the first Reform Act, thanks to electoral registers kept since 1832; but they can only guess how voters cast their votes because of the secret ballot introduced in 1872. The reverse is the case for the historian of the early eighteenth century. Information about the size of the electorate in England and Wales during the years 1701 to 1715 has to be gleaned from a variety of sources.[1] On the other hand poll-books record how a significant proportion of electors actually voted.[2]

The size of the pre-Reform electorate was far from fixed. In his Ford lectures Professor Plumb demonstrated how it grew rapidly during the course of the seventeenth century.[3] This growth was nurtured by both national and local stimulants. In Parliament, 'Country' control of the Committees of Privileges and Elections determined the franchise in several boroughs in favour of a wider number against 'Court' attempts to restrict the electorate.[4] In counties the small but steady increase of the population, coupled with the relative decline in the value of a forty-shilling freehold, swelled the number of voters. Natural growth also occurred in a number of boroughs. In some, growth was forced by the deliberate creation of new votes, for example by splitting burgages or by making more freemen. There were even ways of expanding temporarily the numbers of qualified residents in inhabitant boroughs.

Such stimulants had swollen the electorate in many constituencies during the first half of the seventeenth century. After the right of the Lower House to judge election returns had been conceded by the Crown in 1604 the County opposition used it to extend the franchise in borough after borough. Meanwhile local pressures were also encouraging growth. Consequently, for example, where there had been only 46 voters in Reading in 1625 there were about 900 by 1645, while the electorate of Northampton grew from around 60 to 1000 or so between 1604 and 1661.[5]

In the early eighteenth century the pressures shaping the size of the electorate were not all working in the same direction. At national level the stimulus to growth slackened, and even began to be reversed. Meanwhile, however, expansion in the localities continued almost unchecked.

Between 1701 and 1715 the House of Commons determined the franchise in eleven inhabitant boroughs.[6] In adjudicating between those who favoured a wider franchise and those who wanted it restricted the House compromised between the rival claims once, decided on two occasions in favour of a larger electorate and in every other case resolved that the number of voters should be restricted. There seems to have been some difference between the parties in their attitudes towards these rulings. The Tories favoured a smaller electorate in only three boroughs where the Whigs preferred a larger number, while their attitudes were reversed in the other eight cases.

It appears that the Tories were more suspicious of smaller electorates than the Whigs, since they suspected that they were more susceptible to the blandishments of Whig monied men who were only too ready to debauch the voters from their proper allegiance to local country gentlemen. This basically 'Country' attitude was adopted by the Tories in their reaction to the bribery practised by the New

East India Company in the General Election of January 1701.[7] In March a committee chaired by Sir Edward Seymour presented to the Commons a Bill 'for better preventing bribery and other undue practices in elections, and for preserving the dignity and constitution of Parliaments'.[8] On 3 May a clause was added to this Bill which, if carried into law, would have radically reformed the electoral system 130 years before the first Reform Act. It stipulated that 'in boroughs where are not fifty electors the respective hundred is to join in choosing members'.[9] This clause upheld the Tory view that the forty-shilling freeholders were the most independent and least corrupt holders of the franchise. As the Tories were the party of the landed interest with a strong basis in most counties, this view was not altogether inspired by abstract theories of constitutional purity. The Whigs, on the other hand, as the party of oligarchy with considerably less support in the counties, were more in favour of small, dependent boroughs. Their attitude can be seen in the proceedings during the session 1702–3 regarding the borough of Hindon.[10] The bribery by all candidates at the previous General Election had been so barefaced that a committee was appointed to draw up a Bill to disfranchise the town and transfer its seats to the hundred in which it lay. This Bill passed the Tory Commons, but was dropped in the Lords, where the Whigs had a majority. As long as the Tories could obtain a majority in the Lower House the Committee of Privileges and Elections could put a brake on the growth of oligarchy. After 1715 it was to go ahead unchecked by the legislature.

At local level, on the other hand, the pace of growth quickened between 1701 and 1715 as the manufacture of freemen and the splitting of burgages continued despite parliamentary efforts to curtail them. An attempt to prevent the dividing of burgages by statute in 1696 failed lamentably.[11] Thus the number of people who voted in Pontefract, a burgage borough, climbed steadily, being 130 in 1701, 207 in 1708, 230 in 1710, 250 in 1713 and 264 in 1715.[12] The electorate in Cockermouth grew from 82 to 174 over the same period. Perhaps the most spectacular increase occurred in Weymouth, of which Browne Willis wrote in 1715, 'their number not long since was under two hundred, but within these twelve years, by some late practices, are increased to six hundred and forty-eight or upward'.[13]

The creation of freemen likewise proceeded apace. Between 1700 and 1715 339 were enrolled in Lancaster.[14] At Colchester 125 were created in 1705 alone, 80 of whom lived outside the borough,[15] while on 20 October 1703 59 non-residents became freemen of Dunwich in a single day.[16] Methods of swelling the number of inhabitants of a borough purely for electoral purposes were also developed to a fine art in Anne's reign. A candidate at Hertford in 1710 booked houses and rooms two or three days before the election and lodged in them 'occasional inhabitants', who were called 'mushrooms' by the townspeople.[17] Even the number of freeholders in county elections was increased by means of temporary conveyances which created 'faggot' voters. Reporting the Cheshire election of 1705 Dyer, the High Tory newswriter, complained:[18]

> The Honourable Mr Booth and Crew Offley Esq., set up by the Whig Interest, have carried it by a vast majority against Sir Roger Mostyn and Sir George Warburton, the two late representatives for that county, though the two latter poll'd 300 more than at the former election . . . but this conquest was wholly owing to above a thousand defeasable freeholders that party had made against the election, which is a new and scandalous practice, and if the next parliament do not enquire into it, and put a stop to it, the whole Constitution will be subverted.

That the technique was as novel as Dyer alleged is doubtful, but there can be little doubt that it was on the increase in Anne's reign. In 1712 Parliament took steps to remedy the abuse by passing an Act 'for the more effectual preventing fraudulent conveyances in order to multiply votes for electing knights of shires to serve in parliament'.[19]

The electorate, then, so far from being stable in the early eighteenth century, was still growing rapidly. Professor Plumb gives a conservative estimate for William's reign of about 200,000.[20] As far as it can be ascertained from all the materials relevant to the period it reached 250,700 by 1715. Though this was a privileged 4·3 per cent of the total population of England and Wales, which is estimated to have been 5,826,000[21] – a narrow *élite* by modern standards – it probably represents the widest extension of the franchise before the Reform Act of 1832. After 1715 the national trend, as we have seen, worked against further expansion, while at local level the rate of progress slowed down in the counties and large boroughs, and there was even a distinct shrinkage of the electorate in many small boroughs. Consequently any increase failed to keep pace with the expansion of the population. It is usually estimated that the electorate stood at 435,000 in 1831, though this is possibly on the high side, while the inhabitants of England and Wales as recorded in the census of that year numbered 13,896,797. Thus on the eve of Reform the electorate had dropped to a mere 3·1 per cent of the population.

It is curious that in increasing the number of voters by 217,000 the first Reform Act brought the proportion of the electorate to the total population up to only 4·7 per cent, which was merely 0·4 per cent higher than it had been in the early eighteenth century. When it is borne in mind that the proportion of adult males was almost certainly a good deal higher in 1832 than it had been between 1701 and 1715, then it can be claimed that the electoral system was more representative in Anne's reign than it had ever been before, or was to be again until well into Victoria's.

It was notorious that some Englishmen were more equitably represented than others even in Anne's reign. Geographical anomalies were obvious to contemporaries, Cornwall's forty-four M.P.s being looked at particularly askance. During the Interregnum the Instrument of Government had taken the franchise from many boroughs and given it to some centres where the population was growing. Cromwellian precedents, however, were not popular in the early eighteenth century. Moreover the electorate at that time reflected the distribution of population far more fairly than it was to do later in the century, and the main contemporary complaint was not that the numbers of Members in some localities was disproportionate to the number of people, but that they were at odds with the varying incidence of taxation, which lay heavily on the South and East, and lightly on the North and West.[22]

The right to vote avails little unless one is able to exercise it, and here again the electoral system was more 'democratic' under William and Anne than it later became, for two further reasons: the Triennial Act of 1694 was followed by ten general elections in twenty years, an all-time record; and at these elections there occurred

the greatest number of contests known in the lifetime of the unreformed Parliament. The lowest number of contests in the period
1701 to 1715 was eighty-six, and that was in the 1702 election, for
which an unusually small total is not surprising, considering that it
was the third General Election to take place in eighteen months.[23]
Even this was significantly higher than the numbers reached at mid-
eighteenth-century elections, which rarely totalled seventy, even with
the addition of the forty-five electoral districts in Scotland created by
the Act of Union of 1707.[24] Indeed many constituencies were uncontested for much of the eighteenth century after the passing of the
Septennial Act in 1716. By contrast only thirty were spared a poll
between 1701 and 1715, nine of which were small Cornish boroughs.
In most the voters were able to exercise their right several times at
the seven general elections held in those years. On the whole more
contests occurred in the larger constituencies, there being at least
268 in those with over 500 voters, compared with 239 in the medium-
sized boroughs and only 170 in those with under 100 electors.[25]

These frequent contests gave far more people than the nominal
total of 250,700 the opportunity to participate in general elections
during the early eighteenth century. Quite apart from the addition
of extra voters to the electorate, there was a high turnover of electors
between 1701 and 1715, as can be demonstrated from an analysis of
surviving poll-books.

Given that all voters had to be over twenty-one, a fairly rapid
natural change of electoral personnel might be expected in a period
when the death rate was high. Where the franchise was vested in
property which could be inherited – e.g. in counties and burgage
boroughs – then often the vote might not be obtained until the voter
was well over twenty-one, which would accelerate the natural turnover of electors. Again, transfers of property, especially in burgage
boroughs, where there was strong pressure to purchase burgages in
order to secure political influence, probably accounted more for
changes in the rota of voters than a natural cycle.

Seventy-five burgage-holders voted in Bletchingley in 1710,
only 56 of whom polled again in September 1713. At this rate that
borough was losing on average something like 8·3 per cent of its
electors every years. This was apparently very high, even for a

burgage borough. In Appleby 91 polled in January 1701, 35 of whom voted in 1713, while of the 49 who cast votes at Horsham in December 1701, 22 recorded them again in 1715. These two boroughs had a similar turnover of electors, losing respectively 5 and 4 per cent per annum. By contrast Cockermouth was exceptionally stable, for where 82 men voted in January 1701, no fewer than 60 of them polled at a by-election held there in July 1717, so that only about 1·6 per cent of the electorate dropped out each year.

In corporation and freemen boroughs the composition of the electorate was regulated by political machinery rather than by demographic trends or the property market. Town councils in this period, though annually elected, are often thought to have been self-perpetuating oligarchies. Yet only 18 of the 33 corporation men who voted in Brackley in 1701 were still in office in 1713. Brackley, in common with many other corporations, was in fact undergoing a struggle for control in this period. There were no fewer than 5 disputed elections there between 1701 and 1715. Altogether 50 men voted in them, but they were the last to enjoy that privilege. When the earl of Bridgewater finally gained control of the corporation in 1715 he secured nomination to both seats for himself and his descendants for the rest of the eighteenth century. Struggles to control local corporations also affected the composition of the electorate in freemen boroughs. When the Tories gained control of Orford in 1704, for instance, all those made free since 1693 were disenfranchised, while in near-by Dunwich 49 were struck off the list of freemen on 29 October 1703, which together with the creations of the 20th of that month constituted a virtual revolution in that borough in two days.[26]

The inhabitant boroughs might reasonably be expected to have been more stable, since the franchise in them depended upon a residential qualification. However, the available evidence points to a high turnover of voters even in these constituencies. Thus in Hertford 282 inhabitants voted in 1705, of whom only 223 polled at the next election held three years later – a drop-out rate of about 7 per cent per annum. An almost identical rate of change occurred in Mitchell in Cornwall, where 40 inhabitants voted in 1705 and 36 in 1713, but only 18 polled in both elections. There are several possible

reasons why the 22 names disappeared from the poll-books between
1705 and 1713. The voters might have become politically apathetic
or have been unavoidably absent from Mitchell in September 1713.
However, these explanations hardly account for the appearance of
18 new voters at the second election, and, unless we are to assume
a high death rate in Mitchell, then the conclusion seems inescapable
that there was a highly mobile element among the electorate, such
as is now known to have existed among the population at large during
this period.

Though the restriction of the franchise to forty-shilling freeholders
probably produced more stable electorates in the counties than in
the boroughs, their wider geographical distribution led to a proportionately low turn-out at the polls, and this in turn could mean that
very different voters polled at successive elections. Many forty-
shilling freeholders did not even reside in the county where their
freehold lay. Thus 102 of the 519 who voted in Rutland in 1713
lived outside the county, while 847 of the 3620 Hampshire freeholders
who polled in the same year were also 'outliers', as contemporaries
called them. The problems involved in getting even resident voters
to the polls could be formidable given the distances involved. For
example, some freeholders in Northamptonshire lived nearer to
Oakham, the county town of Rutland, than they did to Northampton.
A contemporary calculated that 6304 Northamptonshire freeholders
had the right to vote. Yet only 4517 took the trouble to do so in
1702, and 4876 in 1705. These figures suggest that virtually the
same electors polled on both occasions, but a collation of the poll-
books shows that in fact only 2875 voted at each.

The forty-shilling-freehold franchise kept the county electorates
reasonably high up the social scale, though their numbers were such
that a substantial proportion of what contemporaries called 'freeholders of the lesser sort' must have enjoyed the right to vote.[27] In
all corporation and most burgage boroughs the franchise was much
more exclusive than this, but in some of the freemen and inhabitant
boroughs the qualification could slip a great deal further down the
ladder. Though Preston, where it apparently descended to the level
of the labouring poor, was unique, in other boroughs it certainly
comprehended shopkeepers, tradesmen and artisans. In London

members of the fifty-six livery companies enjoyed the right to vote
in parliamentary elections, together with the glass-sellers, who were
not of the livery. Some of the livery companies – the Apothecaries
and the Masons, for example – were very select professional institutes.
Others, such as the Weavers and Waxchandlers, incorporated quite
humble citizens. In Norwich the range of voters' occupations was
even wider and deeper. Those who polled there in 1715 were engaged
in over a hundred different pursuits, and included a mathematician
and a poet! Some were quite clearly well-to-do, being described as
freeholders and Gents. Many were employed in the local textile
industry, worsted weaver being far and away the most common
occupation. These and other voters – basketmakers, hotpressers,
soapboilers – were by any test what contemporaries would have
described as 'the inferior sort'.[28]

Most of the London voters in 1710 and Norwich voters in 1715
cast their votes *en bloc* either for the Tory or for the Whig candidates.
Though in London each elector had four votes, and could give them
to any four of eight candidates, the great majority voted for those
put up by one party or the other. In Norwich, where each voter
had two votes, there was so little cross-voting that an enterprising
local printer published two poll-books, one listing those who had
voted for the Tories, and the other showing those who had voted
Whig. Some trades and professions showed a party preference, though
perhaps not as plainly as might be expected. Fewer than half the
London livery companies had a noticeable inclination to one particular
side, and only five gave overwhelming support to one party, the
butchers, barber surgeons, haberdashers and vintners voting fairly
solidly Tory, while the glovers were markedly Whig. In Norwich
party bias is more difficult to detect, except among the freeholders
and worsted weavers, who came out strongly in favour of the Whigs
in the 1715 election.

It would be very dangerous to base any conclusions about social
differences between the rank-and-file supporters of the Tory and
Whig parties on these two constituencies. In the first place they were
very far from being typical, in any sense. Secondly it is difficult to
know what to make of the evidence from them, since it forms no
clear pattern. For instance, the Norwich glovers, quite unlike their

colleagues in the capital, were Tory inclined. But, above all, what makes generalisations impossible is the fact that there was a substantial floating vote in both during the years 1701 to 1715. The Whig vote in London at the 1710 election was one of the lowest recorded in those years, being just over 47·5 per cent of the total cast. In 1701, on the other hand, it had been well over 68·5 per cent. The fluctuations in Norwich were even greater. Between 1708 and 1710 the Whig vote fell from 66·5 per cent to 45·5 per cent.

The twin phenomena of an electorate clearly divided along party lines during general elections and a substantial floating vote between elections were not confined to large borough electorates such as those of London and Norwich. On the contrary they can be detected in every type of constituency, from counties to corporation boroughs.

Surviving poll-books show that where four candidates stood, two on the Tory interest, two on the Whig interest, the votes were usually cast quite solidly in appropriate pairs. Thus in Kent in 1713 the Whigs Fane and Watson collected 2058 joint votes, and the Tories Knatchbull and Hart polled 2656, while only 254 voters cast single votes or 'split tickets'. In the same year in Sussex, where 2838 votes were polled, 1258 voted for the Tories Campion and Fuller and 1060 for the Whigs Buller and Trevor. At Bletchingley two candidates from each party stood in 1710 and 1713. In the first election 76 burgage-holders voted, all but 7 of whom gave both their votes to one side. At the next election 73 voted, and this time only 9 divided their votes between the rival interests.

There are indications that the alignments became more distinct as the period advanced.[29] At Reigate, for instance, in 1701, the Tories Sir John Parsons and Edward Thurland joined against Stephen Harvey and Haestricht James. Parsons's interest in the borough was formidable, and 72 voters gave their first vote to him, but of these only 34 gave their second vote to his partner, while 38 gave it to his rival Harvey. By 1710, however, the interests were much more clearly defined. In that year Parsons stood again, this time paired with John Ward, while James Cocks and William Jordan stood together. One hundred and twenty-one electors voted for Parsons and Ward, 99 for Cocks and Jordan, and only 14 cast their votes otherwise. A similar tendency is observable in Wigan, where there was a fair amount of cross-voting between the four candidates who stood in 1702, and very little between those who contested the borough in 1708.

When only three candidates offered themselves to the electorate the party alignments were often less sharp, since voters were reluctant to throw away a vote altogether. Indeed, the party which put up a single candidate would do so in the hope that voters would give him one vote and distribute their other votes fairly evenly between the two standing on the rival interest, thus polling enough for their man to ensure his return. Even in these circumstances, however, the divisions were not obscured. Often they were actually highlighted by the number of single votes cast for the individual candidate. Three candidates stood in Essex in 1710, Sir Francis Masham and Thomas Middleton together on the Whig interest, Sir Richard Child alone on the Tory side. The outcome was: Masham 2647, Middleton 2678 and Child 3268. The vast majority of Child's votes – 2961 – had been polled singly. At the same time, in Lincolnshire, the Whig George Whichcote stood alone against two Tories, and 'polled between 1300 and 1400 single votes', while another Whig standing on his own in Suffolk had 1800.[30] These 'plumpers', as they were called, reveal in a dramatic way the extent to which the electorate divided along party lines in the early eighteenth century.

The early-eighteenth-century electorate was also extremely volatile. This can be substantiated from figures alone. In Westmorland, for instance, 2305 votes were recorded in 1701 and 2000 in 1702. At the first election 1196 went to the Whig candidates, while at the second the Whigs picked up only 557. In the jargon of the modern psephologist there was a 24 per cent 'swing' to the Tories in Westmorland in 1702. It would be possible to work out the 'swing' in many other constituencies from the numbers polled, as in Hertford, where a Whig majority of 39 votes in 1708 was converted into a Tory lead of 105 in 1710. But the exercise would be almost worthless, since the concept of 'swing' as an explanation of electoral behaviour can be shown to be utterly unrealistic from a comparison of poll-books for different elections in the same constituency. Even when the numbers on successive polls suggest that the electorate remained more or less steady in its political allegiance, closer investigation can reveal a remarkable degree of change. Thus Northamptonshire was contested by four candidates in 1702 and 1705. At the first election the Tories got 4628 votes between them, while the Whigs obtained 4225. In 1705 the Tories polled 4961 votes, the Whigs 4479.[31] From these figures the measurable 'swing' was under 1 per cent. The poll-books for these contests record the votes cast at both by 2875 freeholders. Of these nearly 21 per cent changed their voting behaviour, 248 by transferring one vote, 364 by changing both votes, from Tory to Whig or vice versa. Merely recording shifts in the percentage of votes cast for one party, therefore, does not reveal the true extent to which individual voters changed their party allegiance at elections held in this period. Even in a small borough the degree of inconsistency could be high. Eighteen inhabitants of Mitchell in Cornwall voted in the elections of 1705 and 1713. Of these only 1 gave both votes to the same party on each occasion. 8 voted for a Whig and a Tory in 1705, and for two Tories in 1713, while 9 who cast two Whig votes at the first election recorded two Tory votes at the second. In Brackley, where only the 33 members of the corporation had the vote, the fate of John James's interest shows how fickle some of the smallest electorates could be. James stood there successfully in 1702 but lost in 1705. Eighteen people who voted for him on the first occasion also polled on the second, but only 5 gave him their support at both elections.

Indeed the only predictable blocs of voters were the Anglican clergy and the dissenters. The Tories could rely on the majority of the former, and the Whigs on almost all of the latter.

Contemporaries claimed that the vast majority of the clergy voted Tory in this period. Defoe complained in 1705 that of 318 parsons in Kent over 250 cast single votes for the Tory candidate 'in conjunction with the Papists, Nonjurors and Tackers'.[32] The High-Church newswriter Dyer rather boasted of the clergy's solidarity, noting that they voted as a body on the Tory side at four county elections in 1710, those in Cheshire, Kent, Lincolnshire and Yorkshire.[33] Poll-books bear out these claims. In 1705 107 clergymen voted in Buckinghamshire, 80 of whom polled singly for the only Tory candidate. When a single Tory stood in Essex in 1710, 125 out of 143 ministers 'plumped' for him. Moreover the clergy voted consistently at election after election. In Northamptonshire, for instance, 78 voted in 1702 and 1705, of whom 58 gave both their votes to the Tory candidates on each occasion.

Apart from a few militant Whig bishops and a minority of sympathetic clergymen the Whigs could rely on very little support from the established Church. The dissenters, by contrast, were almost entirely in their interest. In 1710 Dyer observed that 'the Quakers all England over have polled with the dissenters against the Church'.[34] Such claims can be checked in the case of the Quakers, who are sometimes indicated on poll-books because they affirmed rather than swore their allegiance to the Crown. In Hampshire 40 Quakers took advantage of this privilege in 1713, 37 of whom gave their votes to the Whig candidates. In Hertfordshire 73 availed themselves of the concession in 1715, 66 of whom polled singly for the sole Whig candidate.

The fact that the votes of many other electors were unpredictable offers vital clues to the nature of the relationship between the electorate and the political parties in the early eighteenth century. There are two schools of thought about the party allegiance of voters in modern times. One maintains that most voters identify with a political party in their youth and stay loyal to it through their lives. The job of the party agent, therefore, is to see that the faithful get to the polls, since the strength of the parties in the constituencies depends upon the enthusiasm or apathy of their traditional supporters. The other school takes the view that a significant proportion of the electorate changes its vote from one election to another, and that party strength depends upon the number of voters who are persuaded to vote one way rather than the other. Thus where on the first view political conversions usually take place once in a lifetime, on the other they recur regularly.

The evidence from the early eighteenth century emphatically endorses the second view. There were those who voted consistently along party lines at election after election, either through intellectual conviction, such as the Anglican clergy and the dissenters, or through self-interest, such as tenants who obliged their landlords on election day rather than risk eviction. But the extent of the floating vote is phenomenal. It is usually argued that in this period the voters had no interest in the national political struggle, this being confined to

their social superiors. Those who changed sides, therefore, merely
sold their votes to the highest bidder. While there is plenty of evidence
that material considerations influenced electoral behaviour to a considerable extent, it is also clear that in many constituencies voters were
converted from one side to another by events and issues.

Tenants were indeed pressurised. Three of Lord Clare's tenants
who opposed his candidates in the 1713 election at Aldborough were
obliged to quit their farms.[35] But the notion of a submissive tenantry
being dragooned to the polls to vote as their landlords directed is
almost purely mythological, at least as far as the early eighteenth
century is concerned. On the whole tenants were requested rather
than ordered to vote, often with surprising deference. 'I would have
you go round to such of my tenants as are freeholders', Lord
Ashburnham wrote to his agent in Bedfordshire in 1701, 'acquainting
them that I shall take it very well if they all appear and vote for my
Lord Edward Russell and Sir William Gostwick on the election day
as they all were so kind to do the last parliament.'[36] Ashburnham
was being a bit optimistic in expecting his tenants to give both their
votes to candidates of his own interest. The most that a landowner
could reasonably expect was that tenants would reserve one vote for
one of his candidates and dispose of the other as they wished. Even
such modest hopes were often disappointed. Forty-one of Lord
Bulkeley's tenants voted in the Cheshire election of 1710 and as
many as 8 of them did not even oblige him with one vote.[37] Such
insubordination might well have met with reprisals later in the
eighteenth century, but in this period most landlords would think
twice before evicting tenants from their farms. The landed economy
was in such dire straits during the War of the Spanish Succession
that landowners were finding it hard to keep tenants anyway, and
many farms went untenanted for years.[38] In this situation few landowners could afford to be too cavalier in their attitude to tenants
who did not vote as they wished. Lord Nottingham drew attention
to these hard economic facts of life when he addressed the freeholders
of Rutland in 1710:[39]

> Others are terrified with threats of ruin or at least of being turned
> out of their farms, but unless they are frightened out of their wits
> too, as well as their lands, sure such arguments will not prevail.

For as some of you have occasion for a farm, great men have as much need of tenants. God has so ordered this world as that the rich have as much need of the poor as these have of the rich. I am confident these threats will never be executed. These noble persons will not be angry with me for saying they are too wise to ruin their estates. . . .

In some constituencies a voter might hesitate to declare himself at the polling booth through fear not of a magnate but of the mob. There were some counties and several boroughs where party agents were not averse to using mobs in order to intimidate their rivals.[40] The most notorious instance of this practice occurred in Coventry in 1705 when the Tory candidates assembled and armed about five hundred men and proceeded to terrorise any voters who attempted to poll for the Whigs.[41] The employment of unruly elements to assist Tory campaigns was familiar enough for a satirical 'Bill of costs for a late Tory election in the West' to include the item 'For roarers of the word "Church" – £40'.[42] Tory mobs turned out in so many constituencies in 1710 that a Whig complained, 'I am fully satisfied that many peaceable, but faint-hearted, persons declined appearing at the late elections, for fear of broils and bloodshed.'[43] They might well have been deterred from voting in the Westminster election, where a more impartial foreign traveller observed violence on both sides.[44]

Browbeating and bullying, however, were confined to relatively few constituencies, whereas bribery was widespread. There can be no doubt that many electors sold their votes for hard cash or liquor. Some boroughs, especially in the West Country, were notoriously venal, so much so that contemporaries coined the term to 'corn-wallise', meaning to scatter guineas in order to secure an election.[45] They were convinced that the practice was spreading throughout the land. It probably had increased since the Revolution, when the guarantee of the continued existence of Parliament made a seat in the Commons more attractive than ever before.[46] But it had yet to go a long way to reach the degree of corruption practised in the mid-eighteenth century, when a majority of voters were bribed even in constituencies with large electorates. The earl of Clare seems to have begun this practice in Nottingham in 1714.[47] Before that time wholesale bribery was on the whole confined to relatively small constituencies. As a pamphleteer commented in 1704 'bribery and indirect dealings may corrupt electors, yet that cannot extend further than corporations, or small boroughs, for a multitude is not to be bribed'.[48]

Politicians could do better at the polls if they promised rewards in the form of government appointments instead of giving them in the shape of bribes, especially if they looked like being on the side of the majority in the next Parliament, and therefore in a position to dispense state patronage. There were hosts of jobs, particularly in the armed services and the revenue administration, which members of the prevailing side could obtain for loyal constituents. Their abilities to find minor posts for their supporters was a very weighty consideration in the finely balanced interests of Lords Thanet and Wharton in Appleby and Westmorland. In 1701, when the Court's interest was behind him, Wharton's candidates won seats in both constituencies. Shortly after Anne's accession Thanet's steward wrote from Appleby:[49]

> I am glad to hear it's in your power to serve your friends. For the preferring and the placing so many excise men voters and their sons out of this place lately, and promises to others, has very much run down our interest. And 3 or 4 officers or voters that are instructing going about with the gauges daily in this place terrifies and influences them . . .

In the twelve months after William's death Lord Thanet and his colleagues got jobs for at least twenty voters or relatives of voters in Appleby.[50] The total eclipse of Wharton's interest in the first months of the new reign, and the favours bestowed upon Thanet's, were instrumental in carrying all four Westmorland seats for the Tories in the General Election of 1702.

Powerful though the magnetic pull of the Court undoubtedly was,[51] venality was not the sole motive for voting. 'Experience shows', the astute Lord Cowper advised George I, 'that many who have no desire of preferment either for themselves or friends, but live retired on their estates, are yet as hot or hotter than any in these [party] distinctions'.[52] Certainly some of the hottest Tories and Whigs were to be found among the voters at parliamentary elections in this period. During the years 1701 to 1715 a great many electors demonstrated their zeal for a party cause in no uncertain manner. Their response to political issues took a variety of forms, among the more general being letters from groups of constituents to politicians, instructions to newly elected M.P.s, petitions to Parliament and Addresses to the Crown.

Letters pledging loyalty to candidates on the basis of shared principles were occasionally circulated for signature around a constituency. Thus the following round-robin was distributed among the Tory clergy and gentry of Cornwall after being signed by sixty-one of their number at the quarter sessions in 1714:[53]

> Sir William Carew and Mr Travenion having served as knights of the shire for this county, and discharged their trust with all possible honour and integrity, and having at the same time offered themselves to serve again in the ensuing parliament, we whose names are here subscribed, being well assured of their constant and unshaken loyalty for the service of their country in the good old English constitution in Church and State, do declare our resolution to serve them with our vote and interest, and hope that all other well-disposed freeholders will heartily concur with us.

Twenty-two of the leading dissenters in Cockermouth pledged their support for the Whig candidate James Stanhope when he stood there in 1710 by signing a letter to his patron, the duke of Somerset, urging that 'the cause of God's religion and our pure (but poor, distressed Church) calls upon us at this juncture to exert our utmost zeal and hearty endeavour to have good and godly members in the next Parliament'.[54] Seventy-seven citizens of Stroud petitioned a Whig defeated at the Gloucestershire election of 1713, sympathising with his treatment at the hands of 'the friends of France', and urging him to seek a seat elsewhere 'to do what in you lies to stop that mighty torrent which is now coming in like a flood upon us'.[55]

Similar language was employed in the instructions issued to Members of Parliament by their constituents immediately after an election. This technique, first used by the Whigs during the Exclusion crisis, was revived with a vengeance in 1701. In that year at least nineteen constituencies instructed their newly elected M.P.s in

terms which implied that they were delegates rather than representatives.[56] Thereafter the device was rarely resorted to, only a
handful of examples being recorded for the rest of the period.[57]

Petitions, too, fell into disuse after the famous Kentish petition to
Parliament in 1701, which urged the two Houses to stop quarrelling
and to vote supplies for the war. Perhaps the fate meted out to the
Whig petitioners by the Tory House of Commons made this form of
party propaganda less popular than the Address to the Crown.

Certainly Addresses were resorted to with increasing frequency
under Queen Anne. Any event could precipitate their production.
Thus in 1708 the Queen was inundated with Whig Addresses at
the time of the Pretender's invasion, while in 1710 the Sacheverell
affair released another deluge of them, this time mainly from the
Tories. In that year 110 constituencies sent up an Address to the
Queen.[58] A few sent up two, one from the Tories and the other from
the Whigs. But most expressed High-Church sentiments, while
many stressed the Queen's hereditary right so strongly that Lord
Somers was driven to comment, 'by addresses and counter-addresses
there seems to be a kind of listing of men for and against' the
Pretender.[59]

Of course these Addresses did not come about through the spon-
taneous welling-up of public opinion from the grass roots. They
were the products of very careful organisation by party agents. Tories
expressed surprise at the Low-Church Address sent up from
Worcestershire in 1710, and could only conclude that 'there was a
Whiggish Grandjury packed for the purpose'.[60] The rabid Tory
newswriter Dyer dismissed another from Worcester as 'a counter-
address or rather remonstrance . . . signed by presbyterians, anabap-
tists, occasional men, porters, scavengers, journeymen, weavers and
all riff raff that can be procured for love or money'.[61] 'People can't
club to make a wag', observed a Whig pamphleteer in the same year,
'they only sign and deliver. But somebody behind the curtain, whose
meaning they know no more of than they do of Machiavel, turns
'em and winds 'em as he pleases; makes 'em say this is black, that
white, that black, this white, according as the wind sits and he has a
port to make.'[62]

Nevertheless, though they were drawn up by a few committed

individuals, it was felt to be very necessary to make them as representative of the electorate as possible. When the duke of Somerset sent an Address drawn up by James Stanhope to his agent in Cockermouth he urged[63]

> that you and the bailiff will acquaint the whole town therewith, and desire their concurrence to the same. And after you have got it well transcribed upon good paper and the proper title added to it, as you know full well how to do it, that you will desire the burgers of Cockermouth, or as many as you can possibly get, to set their hands to the said address. I know you will do your uttermost to get as many hands as you can to it. . . .

Moreover voters did not subscribe indiscriminately to any Address, for they were well aware that such documents, though ostensibly declarations of loyalty, were really party manifestoes. Thomas Naish, a Wiltshire clergyman, recorded in his diary how the Tory clergy objected to the wording of an Address compiled by Bishop Burnet in 1706, and refused to sign it, joining instead with the Grand Jury.[64] The signatories of Addresses in this period knew that their names would be taken as a kind of party index. Consequently it scandalised the Herefordshire Tories when Nicholas Philpotts signed a Whig Address on the occasion of George I's accession, since they had previously regarded him as being on their side. The recently bereaved Lady Chandos was particularly incensed, and it was with difficulty that Philpotts persuaded her to allow him to be a bearer at her husband's funeral. For, she declared, 'he was a true Church Tory and should be borne to his grave by such'.[65]

The electorate, therefore, was consciously divided along party lines. This was so axiomatic that when the Derby poll-book for 1710 was published, the printer advertised in it that 'all the polls, for the time to come, will be printed in the like manner, to shew the world who are friends to the Church, and who its enemies'. No subsequent poll-book for Derby has survived from this period. Had one in fact been published in 1713 or 1715 it would almost certainly have shown that a significant number of voters who were described as 'friends' of the Church in 1710 were later listed among its 'enemies', and vice versa. At least, 131 voters in this town voted otherwise in 1710 than they had done in 1701, which was roughly 36 per cent of those recorded as voting at both elections. No fewer than 75 of these changed both their votes, 28 voting for two Tories in 1701 and two Whigs in 1710, 47 changing two Whig votes at the first election into two Tory votes at the second. These changes cannot merely be ascribed to venality. A floating vote of this magnitude in a town the size of Derby must to some extent be attributed to a change in political convictions. To what extent remains to be considered.

# CHAPTER THREE

# Party Organisation in the Counties

*I find, however, that the knight [Sir Roger de Coverley] is a much stronger Tory in the country than in Town, which, as he has told me in my ear, is absolutely necessary for the keeping up his interest.*

JOSEPH ADDISON, *The Spectator,*
no. 126 (25 July 1711)

ONE of the main functions of political parties at constituency level is to fight elections. To this end they select candidates, publicise their campaigns, canvass the electorate and arrange that on election day voters who have offered to support them get to the polls. Today these operations are organised by a national machinery, with an official party organisation in most constituencies consisting of a committee and party members. The national party approves candidates, the local committees select them, and the more active party members conduct their campaigns. Because participation in these processes is confined to a small proportion of the total electorate, while at the same time the party machines control the outcome of most contests, those who take part in selection procedures in the major modern parties have been dubbed the 'Selectorate'.

In the early eighteenth century the machinery was nothing like so highly developed. There was no official party organisation, with national headquarters, local committees and fully paid-up members. Nevertheless the workings of the electoral system were in some respects similar.

Between 1701 and 1715 there were Tory or Whig interests in most constituencies. Though these were not organised on a national basis, they were co-ordinated at county level. Informing Thomas

Erle of Whig successes in Norfolk in 1708, Robert Walpole wrote:
'We are so successful in this election that we shall certainly carry
ten out of twelve.'[1] The bishop of Carlisle's predictions for the 1710
election were 'that the county of Cumberland would (as at present)
send up five Whigs for one Tory'.[2] The 1713 results in Cornwall
were particularly gratifying for the Tories. When they were all
known, Lord Lansdowne sent Lord Oxford a 'list of the members
chosen for the boroughs in this county, in which we compute our-
selves to have a majority of ten to one to be depended upon . . . the
largest return of persons particularly devoted to the Queen's service,
and the interest of their country, that ever came from hence, in which
no less than twenty are of my own nomination'.[3]

Electoral managers such as Lansdowne, who backed candidates in
several constituencies, cemented a party interest at county level.
'I may assure her Majesty of the eight members in this county
[Nottingham] for next P[arliament]', wrote the duchess of Newcastle
to the earl of Oxford in 1712, 'though not without great expense,
costing me when at Nott[ingham] castle above £1,000'.[4]

Not that these magnates performed these functions unaided. On
the contrary they were assisted by the efforts of dozens of influential
local politicians. These represented the 'Selectorate' of the early
eighteenth century. Then, more than now, the selection of candidates
was confined to a relative handful of men, while the task of publicising their campaigns, canvassing voters and conveying supporters
to the polls fell to a few hardworking agents.

In the counties the 'Selectorate' consisted of the peers and principal
gentry. The character of each county was to some extent unique
both as to the numbers of politically active landowners and the
degree to which they co-ordinated their activities. In Hertfordshire,
for instance, political organisation was highly formal, as Defoe
informed Harley in 1705:[5]

> The Gentlemen of the Royston Club settle all the affairs of the
> country and carry all before them. . . . There is a monthly meeting
> of the gentlemen of all the neighbourhood the first Thursday in
> every month. They used to drink excessively and do a thousand
> extravagant things, but they behave better now. They have built
> a large handsome square room well wainscotted and painted. . . .

Elsewhere arrangements were more *ad hoc.* In many counties the gentry got together to choose candidates at the assizes or quarter sessions, these being the most convenient rendezvous for country gentlemen, many of whom would be justices of the peace. In Derbyshire before the 1710 election 'at a very great meeting of the Gentlemen at the assizes they did almost unanimously agree upon Curson and Clarke'.[6] In August 1701 Francis Wivel wrote to the earl of Sunderland: 'I am just come from Maidstone Assizes where my Lord Winchilsea, Lord Guernsey, Sir George Rooke and a great party of that side met to carve us out two knights of the shire. . . .'[7] Sometimes public meetings would be specially convened for the express purpose of agreeing upon candidates for a county. Thus four peers and forty-five commoners 'met at the Swan in Warwick the 25th of November 1701 to consult about choosing representatives in parliament'.[8]

In some counties the interest of the Tories was so strong that the Whigs stood no chance, and all that was necessary was to get the Tory gentry to agree. For instance the Tory gentry of Flintshire got together in 1713 and again the following year to agree on an order of rotation for those who aspired to represent them.[9] Denbighshire was another Welsh county 'happy in the good understanding between the principal Gentlemen', while the peace of Carnarvonshire was preserved in 1708 by a 'meeting of the Gentlemen at which all disputes were settled by an amicable agreement'.[10] The Tories were also strong in the English counties, but they controlled only six outright.[11] In others their sway was challenged by the Whigs. When they attempted to nominate the Cornish members at a general meeting of the principal gentry at Liskeard in 1710, the Whigs seceded and set up their own candidates.[12]

When the gentry were thus divided, attempts were sometimes made to reach an agreement between the two parties to avoid an expensive contest. Such an accommodation was made in Buckinghamshire in 1715, though not without a great deal of difficulty as an interesting account of the negotiations amply testifies.[13] That the Buckinghamshire pact was in the end honoured despite the difficulties involved was a remarkable tribute to the party organisations in that county. A similar attempt at an accommodation between the Whigs and

Tories of Cheshire in November 1714 broke down. Although the Tories originally suggested that it should extend for six parliaments, it did not even survive until the General Election of 1715.[14]

Later in the eighteenth century such accommodations became quite common, but in the period 1701–15 it was rare for them to be made, much less to be kept. Indeed Cumberland and Durham were the only English counties in which the parties managed to reach a *modus vivendi* on the basis of sharing the representation equally.[15] In six other counties the Tories virtually monopolised both seats throughout the period, with scarcely a contest to disturb their control. The rest, however, saw a determined struggle between the two sides which frequently erupted into contested elections, not one avoiding going to the polls while some went several times. The Buckinghamshire agreement of 1715 came after no fewer than six contests since 1701, a total beaten only by Surrey and Gloucestershire with seven apiece, though it was equalled by Kent and Sussex, while Bedfordshire, Middlesex and Shropshire came near with five.

When the parties failed to reach agreement, they held separate meetings to select their candidates. Thus Lord Manchester had the leading Essex Whigs round to his house at Leze in December 1704, where they agreed to support Sir Francis Masham and Lord Walden, against whomsoever the Tories might put up at the next election.[16] In 1710 Lord Cheyne arranged a meeting of the Tories at Aylesbury 'to pitch on a fitting person from the Vale to join with Sir Henry Seymour of the Chiltern to oppose Mr Hampden and Sir Edmund Denton in the county'.[17]

Selecting candidates from different parts of a county was a distinct advantage when it came to publicising their campaigns. For it was essential to solicit support from as wide an area as possible, and those selected were expected to make personal applications to as many voters as possible, since the remotest freeholders could influence the outcome of an election, and a candidate ignored them at his peril. In January 1701 Sir Christopher Musgrave scraped home in Westmorland by a mere four votes. At the next election, held only eleven months later, he came bottom of the poll, while his partner Henry Grahme secured his return. Grahme's agent attributed their different fates to Musgrave's failure to make personal application to the freeholders. In a letter to the successful candidate's father he wrote: 'Your son has been very diligent and his behaviour in all things has been to the satisfaction of his friends. I believe your son brought Sir Christopher above 350 votes out of the baronry [the southern end of the county] and if Sir Christopher had appeared in person both had been secure.'[18] One candidate for Norfolk in 1705 took personal application rather far when he rode through the fens 'kissing the farmers' wives and begging their recommendation to their husbands' – in the event he failed to attract sufficient support to encourage him to stand.[19] Not all aspirants for county seats put themselves out to such an extent. James Lowther, when making interest for a Cumberland seat in 1708, told his agent: 'They cannot expect I shall spend much time myself in soliciting since most of the time that my office will allow me to be in the country will be required for looking into my own affairs'.[20] Lowther got away with his indolence largely because no serious rival appeared in the field, and he secured his seat without a contest. When other candidates were busy soliciting votes, however, there was nothing for it but to appear in as many places as possible. Sir Gilbert Dolben told Sir Justinian Isham in the 1705 election that his interest about Peterborough 'suffers much for want of your appearing amongst them. For your adversaries having been there and made their application to everybody of note the freeholders think themselves entitled to the same respect. . . .'[21]

While candidates were expected to make personal applications to the freeholders, they were not left to manage their campaigns single-handed, but were vigorously assisted by the leaders of the appropriate interest in the county. Viscount Irwin's campaign in Yorkshire in 1701 was backed by seven Whig peers besides several country gentlemen of that persuasion. One of them, the duke of Somerset, told him that he had given 'orders to my servants and tenants to obey your commands'.[22] If there was a close poll, the mustering of votes from among freeholders who also held land of the candidate or his backers could sway the result. Analysing the Rutland poll for 1713, when his son Lord Finch had obtained 312 votes, Lord Sherard 300 and Richard Halford 240, Lord Nottingham noted that 38 of the earl of Gainsborough's tenants had voted singly for Sherard, and 40

of the earl of Exeter's for Halford, and commented 'menaces: all
Lord Exeter's tenants, and Lord Cardigan's and Mrs Tryon's'.[23]

In absolute terms, however, the number of voters who were also
tenants was probably small, and the more important contribution of
the political magnates who supported a party interest at election time
was to employ their servants to canvass the county. Both sides made
great use of such agents in Northamptonshire in 1705. Sir Justinian
Isham, a Tory candidate, must have been alarmed to learn that
'Lord Peterborough's steward has been in Northampton this week,
where he treats and is very industrious. They crack of a great
majority of votes they have there, and I doubt not without reason',
and relieved when he heard that 'Lord Exeter put a great deal of
life into your voters by sending out his servants in your cause from
town to town through the whole Soke'.[24]

County campaigns could be directed with military efficiency. In
Kent 'within less than a week after the Assizes, where the candidates
were settled, there was not a parish where there had not been solici-
tations made to engage the freeholders' for the 1713 election.[25]
The Wiltshire Whigs divided their county into areas in 1701 and
made sure that agents were at work in each.[26] 'Ned Baynton will
take care of Melksham and Bromham side,' wrote one agent to
another, 'I will of Calne and Compton. Tom Long and his brother
Dick of Corsham, etc., and do you the same in the North part.'
The Tories in Worcestershire organised their campaign similarly in
1702 on behalf of Sir John Pakington, to whom one wrote:[27]

> I sent a rump of beef and a quarter of mutton to Broadway . . .
> where Ned Goodere had brewed 10 bushel of malt, and Sir H.
> Parker was also there, having sent meat, so that I suppose your
> interest is secured thereabouts. They all drank your health heartily
> and cried out 'a Pakington, a Pakington', nemine contradicente.
> I think it would not be amiss if you sent a letter of thanks to
> each of them, and Sir H. Parker to secure the interest in and
> about Treddenton, and likewise to Ned Goodere who will do the
> same in and about Evesham . . . and I will do it near us. . . .

Entertaining was often a vital incentive to get freeholders to
vote, though prudent men delayed it until after an election, as did
Sir Walter Calverley, who treated about eighty of his West Riding

neighbours who had voted for the Tories at York in 1708.[28] Purses could scarcely stretch to treating a majority of freeholders, however, and exhortation rather than entertainment was the main resource of the electioneer.

Besides making personal visits candidates usually distributed circular letters. A fairly typical specimen was that sent about by the Tory candidates in Middlesex in 1710:[29]

> Being desired by several gentlemen of the county to stand for knights of the shire for Middlesex next election we beg the favour of your vote and interest, and the sooner you engage your friends and neighbours for us the greater will be the obligation to, Sir, your humble servants James Bertie, H[ugh] Smithson.

The opportunity could also be taken to make clear the interest on which the candidate was standing. Lord Scudamore nailed his colours to the Tory mast in the following letter sent to a freeholder in Herefordshire in 1713:[30]

> The repeated favours I have received from you and the other gentlemen and freeholders of this county encourage me to renew my request for your vote and interest at the ensuing election. I am persuaded you expect from your representatives a steady zeal for the Church and Queen, and I desire to continue one of 'em no longer than I comply with these terms. . . .

Such declarations could be remarkably detailed, not only professing the politics of the candidate, but also denigrating those of his opponent. In his letter to the gentry of Cornwall in 1710 George Granville laid down what amounted to a political programme, outlining his attitude to the monarchy, the Church, the Protestant succession, public credit and the war with France.[31] John Speke, when he wrote letters soliciting votes for his son George, who stood for Somersetshire in 1715, accused his Tory opponent Sir William Wyndham of being implicated with Bolingbroke in the making of 'the base and scandalous peace. . . . Had they not made that peace, we had had but some towns before we had gotten to the gates of Paris.'[32] The political content of circular letters reached its most refined, perhaps, in the bogus ones which the Leicestershire Whigs had printed and distributed in 1715,

to discredit the Tory candidates Sir Jeffrey Palmer and Sir Thomas
Cave:[33]

> Sir, your vote and interest at next Election for knights of the
> shire for this county are desired for Sir Jeffrey Pushkin and Sir
> Thomas Thumb being persons of incomprehensible merit and not-
> able abilities to serve their country and zealously affected to the
> present establishment both in Church and State, as far as they are
> permitted by Sir George Bombast [Beaumont] and the honourable
> the Lady Thumb.
> N.B. They are both very quick-sighted, and can take a sign from
> Sir George presently, so that there is no danger of their giving a
> wrong vote when Sir George is in the house.

Such letters were distributed as widely as possible. William Bromley,
canvassing Worcestershire in 1702, 'sent round the country to every
particular freeholder'.[34] This, of course, involved a great deal of
time and trouble, but was standard practice. James Grahme's agent
in Westmorland informed him[35]

> I shall both by myself and son communicate your letter and give
> copies in most parts of the bottom [the northern end of the country]
> but advise your honour to write to all or most of the persons in
> the schedule inclosed, for a letter from your honour's own hand
> has great influence and will make them more active. Your honour
> may hire a hackney clerk to write most of them and only sign them
> yourself.

Some freeholders were very particular that they should receive a
personal letter. James Lowther, soliciting votes in Cumberland,
asked his main agent 'if a body writes distinguishing letters to the
gentlemen of considerable estates and acting justices, I suppose a
common form will serve for most others?' Eventually he found the
task so tedious that he got another of his agents to forge his hand-
writing, hoping nobody would notice the difference. If they did,
and it caused offence, the recipients were to be told that he had not
been well.[36] Westmorland and Cumberland had relatively few voters.
In larger counties no candidate could be expected to write personally
to all the freeholders. John Fleetwood and Richard Greenville
employed clerks to copy 600 letters at 2*d* a letter when they made

interest in Buckinghamshire, while George Lucy actually had a circular printed for distribution in Warwickshire in 1705.[37] Aspirants for seats near London used the newspapers to advertise their campaigns. Thus the freeholders of Sussex were told of the candidature of James Butler and John Morley Trevor for the county seats in the *Flying Post* for 22–25 August 1713.[38]

The London Press was used for electoral publicity far away from the Home Counties. A parcel of Atterbury's *Advice to the Freeholders* was sent to Wakefield for distribution at the quarter sessions to help Sir Arthur Kaye's campaign in 1715.[39] In Worcestershire the Whigs, upon a rumour of a dissolution late in 1703, distributed copies of Sir John Pakington's speech in favour of the Occasional Conformity Bill in order to discredit the Tory knight.[40]

Campaign literature with an even more direct local appeal was also circulated during contests. In 1713 a Whig pamphlet running to forty pages was aimed specifically at 'the Gentlemen and Free-holders of the County of Dorset'.[41] A draft of a satirical Tory broadsheet issued in the name of 'the Gentlemen of ancient families and substantial freeholders of the county of Cumberland' has survived which takes the form of 'a last will and testament' granting their 'dying liberies, properties, privileges and immunities' to Lord Carlisle.[42] Ballads and poems also served their turns in election campaigns. When the Tories Sir Justinian Isham and Thomas Cartwright and the Whigs Lord Mordaunt and Sir St Andrew St John stood as candidates for Northamptonshire in 1705 their names gave rise to a rather tedious Tory 'toast' and a somewhat more entertaining Whig 'reply'.[43] The Leicestershire election of 1715 spawned prolific quantities of propaganda, including two Tory songs.[44] One, 'The Leicestershire Freeholders Song', consisted of nine verses of which the following is a fair sample:

> Thus the Faction combine
> And the Schismaticks join,
> Of our freedoms and votes to deprive us:
> If again they prevail
> With a moderate flail,
> From our Churches and lands they will drive us.

Public spectacle was another way of catching the electorate's attention. In the Worcestershire election of 1705 Sir John Pakington 'had a banner carried before him whereon was painted a church falling with this inscription, "For the Queen and Church, Packington"'.[45] The Church was the chief symbol used by the Tories in public spectacles. In 1710 Dr Sacheverell became the symbol of the Church, and his portrait was prominently displayed at the hustings by the Tories in several counties.[46] The divine's likeness got a rude reception at York, for when 'a great company of boys brought the Dr's picture elevated upon a pole with huzza's, Sir William Strickland turned his backside on't when it was brought before the tribunal'.[47] Though Strickland's gesture was a somewhat isolated one in 1710 when Sacheverell's popularity was at its height, later, when it declined, enough people adopted Sir William's attitude to make a fortune for a manufacturer of chamberpots in the bottom of which the Doctor was depicted.[48] Such was the popularity of Sacheverell in that year, however, that 'in Lincolnshire or Yorkshire (it matters not which) the Gentlemen met in a large plain and distributed fourteen hundred and twelve penny loaves to so many poor people, all marked thus – Sacheverell 1710'.[49]

The Whigs had no symbols to compare in popular appeal with the Tory image of the Church. Occasionally they burned effigies of the Pope or Louis XIV, or carried wooden shoes to represent the social effects of Roman Catholic despotism, but these were stage props left over from the productions of Shaftesbury and the first Whigs, though the effigy of Sacheverell joined the rogues' gallery after 1710.[50] Only once in this period did they hit on a gimmick which was genuinely inspired by a current controversy. This was in the General Election of 1713, which the Whigs fought mainly on the merits and demerits of the treaty of commerce with France which had so divided their opponents that it had been defeated in the previous Parliament. Doubtless hoping to profit from the divisions among their enemies, the Whigs concentrated on this in their campaign, using wool as the symbol of England's staple industry, which, they alleged, would have been ruined if the treaty had gone through. In Wiltshire 'the Whig party appeared (all of them) with wool in their hats at the place of election', and again in Buckinghamshire the Whigs there put wool in their hats, saying 'twas all going into France, and they resolved to keep some on't, before 'twas all gone. Lord Wharton, Lord Bridgewater, Lord Portland and Lord Essex were all at the head of them with wool in their hats: and Lady Wharton with her own fair hands made up several cocars for the country fellows. The Tories had oaken boughs in their hats, and these jokes in their mouths against their adversary that their wits were gone a wool gathering, and that they looked very sheepish, and ba'd them out of the field.[51]

Besides organising spectacles, party managers also made public speeches on behalf of their candidates. Thus is 1710 Lord Nottingham addressed his 'neighbours, friends and countrymen' in Rutland on behalf of his son and Richard Halford, and against the Whig Philip Sherard. Concerning the merits of Halford and Sherard, who had been the knights of the shire in the previous Parliament, he had this to say:[52]

I believe we have all heard that in almost all material questions our two representatives have constantly voted in contradiction to each other, the consequences whereof are that 'tis impossible for both to be in the right, and that we had as good send none to the next parliament as such who perpetually will differ in opinion. . . . Whoever likes the bringing into the nation the Palatines and giving to them all the privileges of Englishmen must vote for Mr Sherard because he gave his vote for that bill, but they who would not bake the bread . . . of our own poor, and give it to strangers, must be for Mr Halford for he was against that bill. . . .

Similar appeals were made to individual voters by party canvassers, as a curious notebook left by one active in the Tory interest in Yorkshire before the 1710 election testifies. This assiduous agent covered Wensleydale and Swaledale, requesting votes from scores of freeholders in those remote regions.[53] Party workers in modern elections will recognise the reception which he met with at Wood End from Roger Talbot's son, who 'told me I was come to the wrong place, for they were all Low Church men thereabouts'.

Electoral agents then as now also had a great deal of trouble in getting voters to the polls. 'My desire of serving you in your election', wrote a Tory agent to Sir John Mordaunt:[54]

did put me upon great difficulties. Our distance from Warwick caused an unwillingness in my neighbours to come. Some wanted horses, some wanted health, some old and wanted strength, which might have been my excuse. I was at that time lame of a leg, which I had unfortunately hurt, and was so sore that I durst not stay to pull off my boot for fear it would not have come on again. I have not put on a boot since that day. I was then forced to use all the horses I could whether fit or not fit. Some were so disabled that they are not yet fit to be used. My neighbours' were some with foal, some had foals and some had none to ride. I was willing to mount as many as I could, that we might discourage our opponents to make such attempts for the future. . . .

Conveying voters to the polls was exceptionally difficult in 1708 when a mysterious disease incapacitated horses.[55] Yet, given the distances which had to be covered and the nature of the transport available, prodigious feats of organisation were achieved by party agents in the counties. The Surrey Tories got round the problem of transportation by arranging for barges to convey voters up the Thames from London.[56] In Warwickshire an ingenious scheme to attract voters to the polls was explained to Lord Sunderland by a Whig agent:[57]

> it might be arranged that for £100 apiece expence in ticketting, which at 12*d* a piece every ticket will engage 2,000 electors who will for double voices be entitled to 2s each, which pays horse-hire from the remoter part of the county or otherwise buys ale, which brings in all the little freeholders that otherwise will not appear. . . .

Some agents were particularly adept at transporting freeholders to the place of election. 'My old gardener's son', wrote a friend to Sir Thomas Cave, 'will I am sure ride a thousand miles to serve me. He has lived there [Leicestershire] these twenty years, and elections are his proper calling. . . . If he meets us at Leicester he may there have your own orders as to the riding out and fetching the country if there is a hard poll, at which he has a most excellent talent. . . .'[58] Some such talented individual must have been hard at work for Conyers Darcy, a Whig candidate in Yorkshire in 1708, since 38 freeholders were somehow persuaded to travel seventy-seven miles from Sedbergh to York to vote for him.

This phenomenon of a whole township voting solidly for the same candidates was a familiar one in the counties, as almost any poll-book testifies. More than half the towns in Cheshire voted over-whelmingly for one side or the other in 1705, the record being held by Budworth Magna, which sent 55 voters to the polls, 53 of whom gave their votes to the Tory candidates.

There is a social explanation for this phenomenon, namely that the voters were succumbing to pressure from the principal landowners in their localities. As we have seen, landlords marshalled the votes of their tenants at election time. Freeholders who did not also lease lands from politically active local magnates might nevertheless vote as they directed, either through deference or prudence. This could account for the fact that out of 64 men from Petworth who voted in Sussex in 1705, 51 supported the Whig candidates, since the leading local magnate, the duke of Somerset, was active in that interest.

However, the subservience of freeholders to the aristocracy and gentry, even if they were also tenants, can be very much overstressed.[59] Towns and villages did not stay permanently attached to the same interest, as they ought surely to have done had the voters in them been at the beck and call of territorial magnates. In 1705 a Tory agent in Northamptonshire wrote to Sir Justinian Isham: 'Everton last election had 34 votes, you had but 6 and Mr Cartwright [Isham's partner] 9, and now I am told you will both have 30. Badby and Newnham will do well so I hope we shall have about 100 votes that were against you last election.'[60] The agent's forecast was sanguine, but not wildly over-optimistic. In the ensuing General Election 21 Everton electors gave both votes to Isham and Cartwright, while only 12 voted for the two Whig candidates. At the same time 35 voted for the Tory partners in Badby and Newnham, and only 18 for the Whigs, where in 1702 the latter had collected 38 joint votes and Isham and Cartwright only 11.

The reason why parishes and towns voted largely for one set of candidates, therefore, was as much political as social. The party agents were faced with the problem of getting the maximum number of freeholders to the polls, many of whom even lived outside the county in which their freeholds lay. Since transport facilities were limited, they were naturally deployed to best advantage in districts where canvassing had indicated substantial support, rather than in

those where it was known that the other interest was overwhelming.
This would be especially true of outlying districts at some distance
from the centre where the election was to be held, since transporting
freeholders to and from the polls could be a lengthy and expensive
business. It cost Lord Clare £172 6s 6d to convey voters to Lewes
in 1715, £32 of which was paid 'to 40 poor freeholders for hiring
people in their absence, and their own loss of time 8 days at 2s. p. day'.[61]

The overall expense of fighting an election campaign in a county
could be considerable. When Sir Thomas Cave stood in Leicestershire
in 1715 an agent reckoned that the final bill would come to £800.[62]
£783 3s 1d was 'paid upon the joint account of Sir Pynsent Charnock
and John Hervey Esq. for the county election' in Bedfordshire in the
same year.[63] Though later in the eighteenth century county contests
were to cost thousands rather than hundreds of pounds, candidates
did not have to expose themselves to expense anything like as frequently as they had done during the period of triennial elections.
Before the Septennial Act gave Members longer security of tenure,
thereby driving up the cost of seats, many counties witnessed a rapid
series of contests which could be financially ruinous for those who
took part in them. 'Elections are so chargeable', complained Sir
Philip Parker after unsuccessfully contesting Suffolk, 'that two are
enough to undo any man.'[64] When one of the Whigs defeated in
Hampshire in 1710 left for Holland shortly afterwards his neighbours
reckoned 'that the elections has been his undoing'.[65]

Not that the candidates were left to foot the bill alone. The local
party leaders met some of the expense for them. Thus Lord Cheyne
contributed substantially to the Tory campaign in Buckinghamshire
in 1713, while George Whichcote, who stood on the Whig interest
in Lincolnshire in 1710, after spending £160 sent bills for £50 to
the duke of Newcastle and the marquess of Dorcester.[66]

Contesting a county, therefore, was essentially a co-operative
enterprise. To choose a couple of candidates from two of several
leading families in itself demanded selection machinery. Publicising
their campaigns, canvassing the freeholders, getting them to the polls,
and sharing election expenses were exercises in party organisation
which reveal that it reached a high degree of sophistication at county
level during this period.

# CHAPTER FOUR

# Party Organisation in the Boroughs

*The parties are now so stated and kept up, not only by the elections of Parliament-men, that return every third year, but even by the yearly elections of mayors and corporation-men, that they know their strength; and in every corner of the nation the two parties stand, as it were, listed against one another.*
BISHOP BURNET, *History of My Own Time* [1708]

WHERE in the counties the party machinery was usually switched on only for an election campaign, in many boroughs it was kept running all the time and demanded frequent overhauling and maintenance. This was because the boroughs were not mere microcosms of the counties, but had their own peculiar problems. Thus although the actual mounting of campaigns bore many resemblances to those in the counties, the careful cultivation of an interest between elections was a feature of party organisation which did not concern county agents to anything like the same extent, and which could even vary from borough to borough.

The methods used to build up or sustain an interest between elections depended to some extent upon the type of franchise prevailing in particular boroughs. In burgage boroughs the most obvious way to do it was to gain control of the properties which carried with them the right to vote. Outright ownership of a majority of burgages was the surest way to gain complete control of a borough under the old electoral system. When investigating the parliamentary representation of Thirsk in this period, the antiquarian Browne Willis noted: 'of the 48 burgage houses about 40 being purchased by Sir Thomas Frankland that were the earl of Derby's makes the electing

2 members in his power'.[1] The duke of Newcastle bought Aldborough
in 1701, which gave him and his family proprietorial rights over the
Members thereafter. At the same time he acquired the nomination
to one of the seats in Boroughbridge. The other seat, however,
remained in the hands of a Tory rival, Sir Bryan Stapleton, throughout
Anne's reign.[2]

When two powerful interests were struggling for control of this
type of borough, burgages were in strong demand. Lord Thanet's
steward in Appleby kept an anxious watch for any properties which
came on the market. The moment they did, he urged his employer
to buy them before they were snapped up by Thanet's Whig adversary,
Lord Wharton.[3] Francis Drake kept his eye similarly on the duke of
Bedford's interest in Tavistock. In December 1711 he wrote to
Sir Peter King: 'I have this day, very foolishly as I think, advanced
£70 upon a purchase within the borough of Tavistock, only to save
2 votes falling into enemy's hands. . . .'[4] Such a keen interest in
burgage properties drove up their market price. The duke of Newcastle
always regretted that his agents had not bought out his rival in
Boroughbridge when it had been possible to do so for twenty-two
years' purchase. After his death his successor was prepared to buy a
parcel of burgages worth £27 6s per annum for £810 – approximately
thirty years' purchase.[5] This was at a time when the normal price
of land was held to be twenty years' purchase, and many estates were
struggling to realise even that.[6] The attractiveness of this peculiar
type of property was made crystal clear in a letter to one of the duke
of Newcastle's agents: 'if his Grace would be pleased to purchase
Sir Bryan's [estate] and mine it would not be in the power of any to
give his Grace the least disturbance here; and to have the disposal
of two boroughs in one parish is what no man in the Kingdom has'.[7]

In theory the corporation boroughs offered the easiest targets for
electoral magnates intent on extending their interests. The number
of voters in them was not only small but fixed. Though usually they
were the leading men in the local business or professional community,
a peer or a country gentleman could reasonably expect them to defer
to him socially. As Thomas Chapman wrote to Lord Fermanagh
with reference to Buckingham, 'your Lordship knows very well
how this Corporation is influenced by the appearance of Gentlemen'.[8]

All that needed to be done was to exploit this respect into submission among a majority of members of the corporation and then persuade them to elect one's supporters to vacancies among their numbers, until the governing body was completely under control and with it the machinery of returning Members to Parliament.

In practice, however, these boroughs were among the most difficult to manage, as Lord Hervey learned from his dealing with the thirty-seven members of the corporation of Bury St Edmunds. His family interest, firmly founded on his estates and country house at Ickworth, just outside the borough, did not need a great deal of cultivation to secure the nomination to one seat. The disposal of charities in the town, gifts of plate, pictures and the occasional dinner to the corporation, seem to have been sufficient for that.[9] Control over the other seat, however, cost him 'much trouble, thought, expence and uneasiness to establish'.[10] This was because Sir Robert Davers, his Tory rival in local politics, had a powerful interest which earlier in the period often overcame his own.[11] Indeed Davers did not concede the fight until after Anne's death, though Hervey had gained the upper hand some time before that event.[12]

In freemen boroughs the outcome of elections could be influenced by the manipulation of the machinery for admitting the name of a freeman to the records. This varied from place to place. In some boroughs membership of a company entitled a man to be entered, in others the eldest sons of freemen could claim their father's status, while in a great many the corporation regulated admissions. Where the corporation controlled the making of freemen, the techniques of building up an interest were an extension of those used in corporation boroughs, the aim being to pack the roll of freemen with the names of one's supporters. John Dibble, a timber merchant of Okehampton, overcame the superior interests of his rivals by making unscrupulous use of the machinery for making freemen there until his exasperated victims felt that nothing less than a petition to Parliament would remedy the situation. This petition throws a great deal of light on the workings of the system in these boroughs:[13]

by the Charter, By-laws and ancient constitution of the said borough, no person can be admitted a freeman without the consent

of the Mayor, and greatest number of the common council:
That upon the death of one of their representatives in parliament,
about 12 months since, Christopher Yendall senior, then mayor
of the said borough, with a few of his accomplices, in a by-room
in an ale-house, without calling the Town Clerk to his assistance
(who is the proper officer for administering oaths) did corruptly
procure 135 persons to be made free of the said borough . . . a
great many of which were servants, waggoners and carters, of
Mr Dibble's, by whom Mr Dibble was chosen. . . .

Methods of managing an interest in inhabitant boroughs could
depend on the precise definition of the residential qualification.
This, too, varied from borough to borough. In Preston the 'inhabitants at large' could vote. Elsewhere restrictions were imposed – in
some the electors were not to be in receipt of alms, in others they
were to be self-supporting householders, 'able to boil their own pot',
while in most they had to pay the local rates 'Scot and lot'. These
variations produced endless disputes in some boroughs about the
customary practice, and the Commons' Journals are peppered with
petitions from disappointed candidates at elections in these constituencies, arguing that unqualified voters had been polled for the
sitting Members, or that qualified voters had been refused who would
have voted for the petitioners.

The most frequent charge in these petitions, however, from every
kind of borough, was that the returning officer had been partial
towards the sitting Members. The support of this official could turn
the most unpromising interest into an unbeatable one. In the last
resort he adjudicated the qualifications of electors at the polls, and,
after the cases of Ashby versus White and the Aylesbury men,
frustrated voters or candidates could scarcely turn to the courts to
redress the damage done by a partial returning officer. These cases
came to the notice of the House of Commons between 1702 and
1704 when the Whig interest in Aylesbury, at Wharton's instigation,
prosecuted a Tory mayor for refusing some Whig votes in the 1701
election. By claiming absolute jurisdiction over electoral disputes,
and imprisoning the Whig voters into the bargain, the House of
Commons in effect left the right to vote to be decided by the prevalent
parliamentary majority, and not by an impartial court of justice.

In most boroughs the duties of the returning officer were performed by the mayor, and because of the strategic position held by this official in the electoral system the party conflict was brought into local elections, even in towns where the corporation did not directly control the electorate. When the recorder of Shaftesbury, an inhabitant borough, died, the Whig interest took pains to get him replaced by one who 'is not listed in the Tory band of gentlemen'.[14] Lord Wharton clinched his nominee's interest at Appleby in 1708 by himself obtaining the post of mayor in that burgage borough.[15] The importance attached by the Whigs to procuring friendly mayors for the 1713 election is vividly illustrated in an urgent letter which Lord Lansdowne penned to the earl of Oxford:[16]

> Mr Vincent and his son are going tomorrow for Cornwall to be present at the election of a mayor for the town of Truro where we are in danger, or rather, under a certainty of losing both members at the next choice for a Parliament unless your Lordship is pleased to give your assistance. I have appropriated every penny of my own rents in that county for service of this kind, being attacked in every corporation. It is not to be imagined what efforts have been made, and what money has been lavished upon this occasion. The contention and expense is greater than ever was known upon the choice of a Parliament, so much the enemies of the Government have thought it necessary to be before hand with us in securing returning officers.

These struggles became particularly intense when they involved Churchmen on the Tory side and dissenters on the Whig, as election petitions testify. At the hearing of one from Wilton in 1702 a witness claimed that 'he had heard the Mayor say that he would make none burgesses that were not Dissenters from the Dam's Teat'. In the words of a Tory vicar, 'this alarmed the zeal of a Church of England Parliament, and though I do not say it was the ground and occasion of bringing in the Occasional Bill, yet, no doubt, it was a great motive to quicken their preparation of it'.[17]

The Occasional Conformity Bill was designed to smash the dissenting interest in corporations, and thereby to damage the Whig interest. When it became law in 1711 it certainly had this effect in some constituencies. The Whigs lost control of Coventry in 1712 when sixteen members resigned from the corporation as a result of

the Act.[18] The poor performance put up by the Whigs at the 1713
election in many boroughs where they had previously contrived to
hold their own was due to a convergence of many pressures, but
among them should be included the final success of the Tory drive
against dissenting corporation men.

In Portsmouth the struggle for control between Churchmen and
dissenters was so fierce that it led to the emergence of rival bodies
both claiming to be the legitimate corporation. How this happened
was explained in a Tory account of the contest:[19]

> such have been the divisions in this corporation for many years
> past that the mayor and aldermen could not agree in filling up the
> vacancies of alderman, so that at the death of Nathaniel Harford
> the mayor which happened the 10th of December 1709 the
> number was reduced to seven . . . upon the death of the said
> Harford they met and chose Joseph Whitehorne mayor. This
> Whitehorne (who never qualified himself for that office) with the
> concurrence (only) of Seager and White (who are as great dissenters
> as himself and not qualified for the place of alderman) and John
> Thomas (who is a madman) did elect six aldermen and forty
> burgesses in order to secure the election of a mayor fit for their
> purposes so as to choose members to serve in this Parliament and
> for ever blast the hopes of the honest Church of England members
> of the corporation. . . .

Portsmouth was not the only borough in which the party conflict
splintered the corporation into two bodies during the period 1701–15.
In Brackley, Buckingham, Camelford and Marlborough, for example,
the jockeying for positions by Whigs and Tories led to the formation
of rival corporations.[20]

All the groundwork put in between elections – the buying of
burgages, the cultivation of the voters, the struggles to control
corporations, the efforts to secure partisan returning officers – was
labour in vain if it was not followed up by a good campaign. In the
boroughs, as in the counties, candidates had to be selected, votes
canvassed and a good turn-out organised on election day if there was
a contest.

In large boroughs selection procedures could be quite formal.
Before the 1701 election in London 'a great number of the Whiggish
party met at the Crown tavern behind the Exchange and agreed to

put up Sir Robert Clayton, Sir William Ashurst, Sir Thomas Abney and Mr Gilbert Heathcote'.[21] The Coventry Whigs worked out an elaborate order of priority for potential candidates in 1705, as George Lucy explained to the earl of Sunderland:[22]

> As to the affair at Coventry there has been some rubs in the way as to the persons proposed (being Sir Orlando Bridgeman and Mr Hopkins junior), the latter not being inclined to spend monies and the former not willing to be at any charge likewise unless he might be assured of the preference in the election, which Mr Hopkins as I have been informed was not willing to comply with. Since which there has been another project set on foot with Mr Hopkins senior's consent, by which it is proposed to Sir Orlando Bridgeman and Sir Fulwood Skipwith to accept of what interest can be made, and in case Sir Fulwood refuses then it is offered to Sir Francis Dashwood, Sir Orlando's father-in-law, or any other person Sir Orlando shall prevail with to join him.

In most boroughs, however, there was no need for formal agreements, since certain families had such dominant interests that candidates recommended by them were adopted without question. There was no hint that the approval of anybody else would be necessary when the duke of Somerset wrote to ask Paul Methuen to stand at Marlborough: 'I take this way to know if you will appear in that borough on my interest, which shall be entirely at your service. I have very good reason to believe we shall be successful or I would not appear in it.'[23] Proximity of country houses to boroughs, such as Somerset's seat at Maiden Bradley, near Marlborough, Sir Edward Seymour's at Berry Pomeroy near Totnes and John Aislabie's at Studley Royal just outside Ripon, gave their owners a considerable interest in those boroughs. 'The most desirable property now for sale,' Governor Pitt was informed in 1708, 'perhaps in all England, is Clarendon Park and the manor of Christchurch . . . the proprietor controls the elections of burgesses of Christchurch.'[24] The Hon. James Brydges, who was looking around for a desirable country seat in the same year, was advised to try Laycock in Wiltshire because 'Chippenham is next parish, which is now governed by Mr Montague of Lockham, whom you know in the House of Commons. That borough which is not so venal as many are will be glad to have the honour of Mr Brydges' favour, if ever he settle at Laycock.'[25]

c

Though it paid to be of local standing, a would-be candidate could invade a borough from outside and create an interest independent of that of the local magnates by spending money freely on the voters. An assumption made by many Tories was that they were more representative of local interests, and that the Whigs were especially guilty of carpet-bagging. The country gentlemen who subscribed to Dyer's High-Church newsletter would be shocked but not surprised by the wild rumour he circulated in the 1705 election that '17 strangers are like to be chose in Wiltshire, not one of them having a foot of land in that country, to the reproach of the electors, for not having a greater value for the honest, loyal neighbouring gentry'.[26] Dyer's implication that only unscrupulous Whigs would set up carpet-baggers was shamelessly one-sided, considering that the record for multiple candidatures in this period was held by Jack Howe, a notorious Tory, who stood in no fewer than four constituencies in 1702 – Bodmin in Cornwall, Gloucestershire and Gloucester, and Newton in Lancashire – and was returned in them all. Howe was prudently insuring against failure, having been beaten in the previous election. Some Tackers were offered similar security in 1705 when the electoral tide was flowing against them. According to the *London Post* 'so rank was the spirit of the high party in this county [Suffolk] that having but one honest gentleman chosen before at Ipswich . . . rather than he should be in the House again, they send up to London for one of the rankest Tackers . . . though they never saw him before in their lives'.[27]

Leading Tories who failed to get into Parliament could be offered safe seats in constituencies where they were unknown, but they were notably less successful in such rescue operations than were the Whigs, who had fewer scruples about invading boroughs with outside candidates.[28] Indeed the Whiggish new East India Company was guilty of the most barefaced carpet-bagging during the General Election of January 1701. Country gentlemen were outraged by the invasion of City men into provincial boroughs. When the Parliament met, Samuel Shepheard, the leading promoter of the company's election campaign, was accused of bribery in six constituencies: Andover and Newport in Hampshire, Ilchester in Somerset, Bramber in Sussex, and Malmesbury and Wootton Bassett in Wiltshire.

These were all boroughs with small, corruptible electorates, while
their geographical distribution testifies to the wide scope of Shepheard's
electoral activities. The incensed squires found him guilty of bribery
and expelled him from the House.[29] After his disgrace it was widely
believed by the Tories that the City had its own funds earmarked for
fighting elections on behalf of unscrupulous Whig businessmen intent
on purchasing a seat in Parliament. Henry St John in a debate on the
Property Qualification Bill stated that 'he had heard of societies that
joint'd stocks to bring in members'.[30]

The idea that monied Londoners could foist themselves unbidden
onto provincial boroughs gave the Tory gentry nightmares, but there
is little evidence that it was practised on a scale large enough to
justify St John's allegations. Few Whig carpet-baggers were as bold
as William Cotesworth, a City merchant who contested a by-election
at Boston in 1711: 'Mr Cotesworth was not known in town, until
he came . . . there was afterwards in the town a great plenty of a
new liquor, they never had there before, called whistle-jacket,
brought from Grimsby by the carrier, and was made up of brandy
and treacle. . . .'[31] Cotesworth's technique of by-passing the local
magnates by pouring drink down the poorer voters' throats was
outside the realm of practical electioneering in all but a handful of
boroughs.

When putting themselves forward for election those candidates
were at an advantage who could show or offer some benefit for the
constituency or individual constituents by their returns. The advantages which an M.P. could bestow on his electors were many, from
merely franking their letters so that they went post-free, to obtaining
lucrative posts for them in the revenue administration or the armed
forces. He could also look after the interests of the constituency as
a whole should any measure crop up in Parliament which affected it.
Peter Shakerly and Henry Bunbury made great efforts to safeguard
the interests of the Chester tanners against the effects of the duties
placed on leather in the years after 1711.[32] The Members for
Nottingham were urged in 1702 to do all they could against the Bill
to make the river Derwent navigable.[33] In this respect sitting
Members were better placed than aspiring Members, who could
only accuse the existing representatives of neglecting its interests, or

promise to look after the constituency if elected. Thus Edward
Gould wrote to Exeter corporation to offer himself as a candidate:[34]

> tis neither vanity or ambition that are the motives to my request,
> but an earnest desire to be in such a capacity that I may in a
> proper station promote the weal and flourishing of Exeter, and
> think of some cordial that may revive and increase our trade that
> long has languished under the manage of ignorance, or neglect. . . .

More important than offers of material advantages were declarations
of political allegiance, for local party managers carefully vetted the
politics of candidates who requested their interest. In 1710 the
bishop of Worcester vouched for the sound Whig credentials of
'Mr Walmisley, Chancellor of Lichfield, whom I have persuaded
to stand at this election for burgess of that town in parliament. Of
all that are likely to be chosen in that place he is the only man that
I know will do her Majesty or the Church of England faithful
service if he be chosen. And the choosing of him will keep out one
of the two that are both in the opposite party'.[35] Lord Cowper,
recommending a relative to the duke of Newcastle, assured his grace
that 'he may be depended upon as perfectly honest and steady in the
public business'.[36]

If the behaviour of Members in the House did not live up to the
expectation of those who had sponsored their elections, the support
of their sponsors could be withdrawn. 'I hear Sir Michael Biddulph
does not vote along with you in the House,' Lord Stanhope wrote
to Thomas Coke in 1702, 'and if it be so he must expect to lose my
interest for the future.'[37] When the duke of Beaufort heard that
his nominee at Bath, William Blathwayt, had voted against Dr
Sacheverell, he made interest against him in the 1710 election.[38]
How demanding patrons could be in this respect can be seen from
the fate of Charles Leigh, Lord Brooke's nominee at Warwick.
Referring to Leigh, William Bromley observed to Robert Harley,
'an honest gentleman near me (who behaved himself unexceptionably
in all other respects) has suffered so much in his interest that he
will scarce recover it, upon a report that he withdrew at the first
question the last session upon the duke of Marlborough, because he
could not think the taking of the bread money illegal, though he
agreed it to be unwarrantable'.[39]

Once a candidate had been approved, the next step was to publicise his candidature. If no contest threatened, canvassing could be kept down to a minimum. It was not even necessary for the candidate to canvass in person. When no serious opposition was in sight at Hereford in 1710 the Hon. James Brydges wrote to a friend 'my interest is so sure that there will be no necessity for me to take a journey down to be chosen'.[40] It was, however, considered courteous to visit a borough, even if the election was to be a formality. Newton in Lancashire was the pocket borough *par excellence* in this period. Yet though the patron, Peter Legh of Lyme, could guarantee the return of his nominees, he asked them to solicit in person if they could 'to prevent some sort of censures that formerly has been made . . . that Newton members seldom was known to the voters'.[41]

If the other party was making interest too, however, then personal application was considered to be essential. When the duke of Somerset approached Paul Methuen to stand at Marlborough, he stressed that 'it will be absolutely necessary that you do go thither'.[42] There were many reasons why James Stanhope lost his election at Westminster and nearly lost his seat at Cockermouth in 1710, but one of them was the fact that he was unable to solicit personally, even though his absence from England was occasioned by his being a prisoner of war in Spain. When James Brydges's interest in Hereford was threatened in earnest in 1708, he reacted with none of the complacency which he registered two years later. At the first warning of danger he panicked, and rushed down to Hereford, actually arriving there before the end of the parliamentary session. On reaching the city he became so alarmed at the reports of his opponent's strength that he took out an immediate insurance policy by persuading the Lord Treasurer to bring him into Parliament for a safe Cornish borough in case he lost his election at Hereford.[43]

Attempts to avoid a contest by coming to terms with the opposing interest were even rarer in boroughs than in counties. Indeed there is only one recorded example of a negotiated accommodation. On 5 July 1707 'articles of agreement' were drawn up 'between Sir Richard Farington, baronet and John Farington Esq. on the behalf of one party, and Sir John Miller baronet and Thomas Carr Esq. on the behalf of the other party, for maintaining and preserving the

peace of the City of Chichester'.[44] They consisted of eleven clauses
which made elaborate arrangements for sharing the representation of
the borough both in Parliament and on the corporation. Despite the
solemnity of the pact it was a dead letter from the start, a contest
taking place in Chichester at the subsequent General Election.
There is evidence for informal pacts operating in other boroughs.
Sir John Cropley, a Whig nominated by the earl of Shaftesbury, and
Edward Nicholas, a local Tory standing on his own interest, arrived
at an understanding in Shaftesbury for several years. It nearly ended
in 1708 when an independent Whig tried to come in there, much
to Lord Shaftesbury's annoyance, and it did break down in 1710
when two Tories were returned.[45] Judging by the politics of those
returned from other boroughs, the two parties appear to have kept
the peace and avoided contests in only three between 1701 and 1715.[46]

Elsewhere the appearance in the field of rival candidates usually
meant a hard-fought campaign, with both sides canvassing and treating
the voters. Door-to-door canvassing and public addresses were then,
as now, the main tactics in the campaigns of most candidates. Lord
Wharton sent a letter to his agent in Cockermouth in 1708 recommending Albemarle Bertie, 'which he communicated to the Burghers
by going from house to house and eating and drinking for a week
together'.[47] Lord Thanet's agent went round Appleby in 1713
'to caution the voters not to be ingaged, but to reserve their voices
for . . . such as were zealous for the Government and Church'.[48]
The imperious duchess of Marlborough took personal application to
extremes when she granted audience to several electors of St Albans
in her efforts to promote the Whig interest there in 1705, being
accused of upbraiding those who declared themselves to be in the
opposite camp by saying that 'it was the Queen's desire that no such
men should be chose, for such men would unhinge the Government;
and the Papists' horses stood saddled day and night, whipping and
spurring', while 'Tackers would be injurious to the Government
and were for the French interest'.[49]

Intensive canvassing could be an exhausting business, as John
Chetwynd discovered at Preston. Reporting on the progress of his
campaign there, he wrote, 'but more of this when we meet, if this
d[amned] parliamenteering does not kill me. For I am half dead

already what with drinking, smoking and walking the streets at all hours . . .'50 Electioneering could be so gruelling that when William Bridges was asked to stand at Weobley his father urged him to refuse: 'I do not think your constitution able to stand the fatiguing debauchery of a poll or any other contested election.' When his son expressed his determination to proceed, he advised him to engage agents to help him, but warned him: 'There is no going to Weobley for any agent without money in his pocket to set taps a-running in the public houses, and a large sum to deposit in a safe hand as a certain reward and purchase for those votes you can be promised.'51

Treating and bribery were essential lubricants for a local party machine. A bill preserved among the duke of Somerset's papers at Cockermouth itemises expenditure on food and drink at a by-election held there in 1711 which came to £26 13s 5d, no less than £16 3s being spent on wine, brandy and ale.52 Candidates had to be careful how and when they paid voters for their support, however, since treating after the *teste* of the writ calling an election was illegal. Judging by the petitions upon controverted elections, the law was more honoured in the breach than the observance. Almost any petition provides details of such irregularities.53 Some candidates were unusually enterprising – at Carlisle and Shrewsbury, for example, orders were placed for vast quantities of shoes from the local shoemakers.54 But such enterprise was rare, and for the most part the accusations and counter-accusations of giving small sums of money to innumerable individuals, or pouring rivers of ale down countless throats, become tedious and even a little depressing.

This biased evidence has, moreover, to be used with great care. It gives a distorted view of the methods used to gain or maintain an interest in this period. Quite apart from it being the testimony of interested parties, the whole point of these petitions was to draw attention to irregularities. Yet they are often cited as evidence for the normal working of the electoral system. The resulting impression is overwhelmingly sordid, venal and corrupt. When checked against more objective evidence, however, a rather different picture emerges.

Take election expenses, for example. These were often alleged to cost thousands of pounds. Contests in some of the larger boroughs could be as expensive as a county campaign. John Chetwynd spent

at least £850 unsuccessfully fighting Preston in 1715, while in the
same year John Plumtree and George Gregory ran up a bill of
£864 19s 8d in order to secure their returns for Nottingham.[55] Seats
in the medium-sized and small boroughs, however, seem to have cost
appreciably less. Sir Stephen Fox's campaign at Cricklade set him
back £308 2s 4d in 1701, which was possibly on the high side for a
borough with 100 or so voters, since Lord Bruce paid only £200 to
obtain a seat at Bedwin, reputedly one of the most venal boroughs of
that size in England.[56] In such constituencies a candidate would
probably have to budget on spending in the region of £100–£200.
James Grahme spent only £56 contesting Appleby in 1701, but he
failed to obtain a seat. In 1702, when he was successful, he parted
with £150. Gervase Pierrepoint, who was successful on both occasions, spent £120 at the first and £180 at the second.[57] Even such
sums, relatively small compared with election expenses later in the
century, were enough to put some potential candidates off seeking
election to Parliament during this period. When Charles Aldworth
was approached by the duke of Northumberland to stand at Windsor
he replied:[58]

> should the case in truth require the help of money to be spent,
> though I can assure your Grace I have different accounts from
> Windsor, it is by no means what suits my circumstances. I thank
> God I have wherewithal to maintain me with comfort and some
> credit in the world, but to engage myself in debt by elections is
> what I cannot think of. I have too long felt the heaviness of debts,
> and now I am upon the point of coming out of that very grievous
> condition, it would be thought madness for one upon uncertainties
> to venture again into that sea of miseries.

Candidates in early-eighteenth-century elections appealed to the
principles as well as the purses of the voters even in boroughs. Thus
'Phil Ecclesiasto' addressed the voters of Cockermouth in 1710:[59]

> We can't but be very surprised and concerned to hear that a man
> of your temper, sense, and (as we hoped) well affected to the
> Established Church should at this time so far start aside as to
> associate with separatists and schismatics and assisting of them in
> the choice of members for the next British Parliament . . .
>     Though his Grace my Lord Duke [of Somerset] himself (who

has been a very bountiful benefactor to your borough) should now knowingly recommend to you a person of republican principles, one that would not allow her present Majesty any hereditary title, that would be for clipping and paring the prerogative of the Crown, and for the erecting new schemes of government in order to ruin and undermine our present happy constitution and establishment in Church and State . . . can you think yourself under any obligation to make choice of men for your representatives whom you have any reason to fear are of such dangerous principles?

Sometimes candidates distributed distinguishing marks to their supporters. The Whig brewers Cox and Cholmley decked their draymen out in grey hats with red ribbons when contesting Southwark in 1702,[60] while at Honiton in 1705 'the two parties . . . were very nicely distinguished. . . . Buff was the symbolum of the Whigs. These had box in their hats, doors, windows, the other had laurel leaves . . . and on the day of the election the Gentlemen who came in with Sir W. Drake had a little knob of shoemaker's thread in their hats to show that they were Tackers.'[61] At Newcastle upon Tyne the Tories in 1710 'had red and blue favours in their hats with this motto in letters of gold, vizt: for the Queen and Church.B.W. [Blackett and Wrightson]'.[62] The Whig wool motif was used in some boroughs as well as in the clothing counties in 1713.[63] In Liverpool, as a variation on the theme, they gilded their hats with tobacco.[64]

The intensity of party feeling, even in small boroughs, could be very high. Few Whig canvassers would have cared to solicit support in Queenborough, where there was an electorate of under seventy, after the fate which overtook Michael McClellan there in 1705. McClellan was a Scot resident in the borough who tried to prevent the re-election of Robert Crawford, a Tory who had voted for the Tack. He therefore went about the town 'expressing much zeal against the Tackers, of whom he had a list which he showed to several people'.[65] Crawford, who was governor of the near-by garrison of Sheerness, was absent at the time and another officer, Major-General Winsly, took it upon himself to teach the Scot a lesson. He paid a soldier of the garrison, Joseph Dalton, half a crown 'to beat him a little for his sauciness', but unfortunately Dalton did his job too well, being 'so devilish as to knock his brains out'.[66]

Dalton was charged with McClellan's murder, and sentenced to
death at Maidstone assizes in July 1705, though Major-General
Winsly, who was accused of being an accessory, was cleared by the
jury. While the case lasted it attracted considerable attention, the
Whigs taking the side of the murdered man, the Tories accusing
them of trying to incriminate the major-general. As Dyer put it,
'the same was a mighty party cause'.[67]

Careful canvassing enabled election managers to predict the likely
outcome of a contest, and thereby to decide whether it was worth
while to carry on to a poll. After sparing 'neither pains nor expense'
at Preston, John Chetwynd reported to Lord Finch, 'I had the
honour to acquaint you in my last that I had not above 150 voices
out of 900 and odd. I have since increased my number to near 200
and hope to get some more, but I question if I shall get enough to
make a majority. . . .'[68] In the event his prediction proved correct.
When Nicholas Philpotts campaigned in Hereford his prospects were
very carefully calculated by Lord Chandos, who had long experience
of the borough. At the outset of Philpotts's campaign he reassured
him:[69]

> I can't see but that, if you can depend upon the number promised
> you, you must carry it. For allowing 700 freemen in the City,
> and 200 in the country, in all 1800 votes. Deduct out of those
> 120 which you have single, there remains 1680. Deduct again
> 300 from the 150 reserved, there then remains 1380, the third
> of which is 460, whereas you have promised you 480, besides 40
> and 50 you shall certainly have from London. And as for the
> reserved 150, which are 300 votes, you write you have a chance
> for your share of those, and have already upwards of thirty promised.
> So that upon the whole, I shall be glad you don't think of desisting,
> and conceive great hopes that you'll carry it.

Getting the voters to the polls in a large borough like Hereford,
where many lived in the country and even in London, required
careful organisation. James Brydges relied on his agent, Francis
Woodhouse, to convey freemen from as far away as Worcestershire
and Monmouthshire, and to pay their expenses.[70] Similar arrangements must have been necessary in other freemen boroughs where
voters were 'foreigners'. Owners of burgages, too, often lived away

from their constituencies. Of the 150 who voted at Reigate in 1713, only fifty-five lived in the town.[71] In most boroughs, however, persuading voters to turn out was a relatively much easier task than that which faced party agents in counties.

An election campaign, however, as we have seen, was but the tip of electoral activity in parliamentary boroughs. Interests had to be carefully cultivated between elections by a variety of techniques peculiar to individual boroughs. The snapping up of burgages, the organisation of council elections, the creation of freemen and the bribing of inhabitants had all to be sedulously supervised. These activities were prosecuted ceaselessly by party agents in the boroughs, ready for a sudden dissolution of Parliament, which could be expected at any time during this period. Having anticipated it, the parties would not be at a disadvantage in waging an immediate election campaign on behalf of their candidates. The efficiency with which so many boroughs fought so many contests at seven general elections in fourteen years is a tribute to the state of preparedness in which the party machines were kept during the period 1701 to 1715.

# CHAPTER FIVE

# The Safe Seats

*Few men attempt . . . rash measures but such as are almost*
*certain of being elected again, either by the prevalency*
*of their party, or the absolute dependency of their cor-*
*porations. . . .*

HENRY ST JOHN to the DUKE OF MARLBOROUGH,

25 May 1705

DESPITE an unparalleled run of general elections and a fierce
struggle between the Tory and Whig parties in the constituencies,
some 189 of the 513 seats for England and Wales were held by
members of the same party between 1701 and 1715.[1] Over a third
of the English and Welsh seats, therefore, can retrospectively be
regarded as having been 'safe' during those years. Although this
might appear to have been on the high side, it was in fact far less
than the proportion retained by the Conservative and Labour parties
in modern times. Between 1955 and 1966 547 constituencies in
England and Wales returned one Member to Parliament. Of these,
no fewer than 394 sent members of the same party to Westminster
at each of four general elections held during that period, elections
which produced the highest Conservative majority since before the
Second World War, and the greatest number of Labour M.P.s
since the electoral landslide of 1945.

Where the major parties nowadays contest almost every constituency, however hopeless the outlook, the Tories and Whigs of
the early eighteenth century rarely fought elections if they stood no
chance at all. Consequently from 1701 to 1715 there was a definite
connection between the number of safe seats and the incidence of

contests. For instance, two-thirds of the Welsh seats were safe, while there were only twenty-nine contests in Wales between 1701 and 1715. It is true that the incumbents of some seats survived several assaults from their opponents. Thus the Whigs tried three times to break the Tory control of Somerset, while the Whig brewers Charles Cox and John Cholmley fought no fewer than five contests in Southwark between 1701 and 1710 and survived them all. Eventually Cholmley was removed by death and Cox stood down. The electorate of Southwark was so Whiggish that it returned two Whigs to Parliament after each of eight contests which took place there between 1701 and 1715. The Tories managed to sneak a seat there only by petitioning the Tory House of Commons after a by-election in 1712.

On the whole there was a higher incidence of contests and a lower proportion of safe seats in the large constituencies than in the medium and small boroughs. Boroughs with over 500 votes accounted for only 32 safe seats, while those with electorates of under 500 provided 120. It was phenomenal for a borough the size of Southwark, therefore, with 3500 voters, to retain its party loyalty through so many elections. Safe seats in other large boroughs were usually uncontested. Thus the hold of the Tories Peter Shakerly and Sir Henry Bunbury over Chester, where there were about 1000 voters, was such that they were never opposed after 1701.

The Tories indeed had substantially more safe seats at their disposal than their rivals during this period. Throughout the years 1701 to 1715 they held 114 safe seats whereas the Whigs had only 74. The Tories were particularly strong in the counties, controlling 31 shire seats to the Whigs' 5. This adds substance to the claims made for the Tory party during the reign of Queen Anne that it had a natural majority in the country.

Six English counties returned two Tories throughout the period, while none was completely controlled by the Whigs. Tory control of both Devon seats was so assured that the Whigs never challenged it, while in Derbyshire they withdrew from the unequal struggle after losing in 1701. At that contest the combined interests of the dukes of Devonshire and Rutland, whose eldest sons put up on the Whig side, were unable to overcome the support given by the bulk of the

gentry to the Tory candidates. The competition between an aristo-
cratically led Whig interest and a gentry-dominated Tory interest
was a feature of other county contests besides this one in Derbyshire.
After surveying the role of the peers in parliamentary elections
during the reign of Queen Anne, Geoffrey Holmes was led to the
conclusion that 'there were many counties where the Whigs depended
for their main strength on a group of titled grandees. Within the
Church party, however, the aristocratic confederacy was not only a
rarer phenomenon; its comparative importance was also notably less.'[2]
Thus in Yorkshire, 'though all the chief aristocratic landowners were
Whigs, the party never gained more than 1 seat during Anne's reign',
while in Sussex 'the Tory gentry more than held their own against
a powerful array of Whig peers'.[3] It was the solid Toryism of most
country gentlemen which enabled the Tory party to control so
many county seats. As one contemporary put it, 'the majority of the
gentry upon a poll will be found Tories'.[4] When the same could be
said of the clergy it is little to be wondered at that the Tory party
had so many more safe seats than the Whigs in the counties.

It was largely their sway in the counties that gave the Tories
such a commanding lead over their rivals in the possession of safe
seats. The only other type of constituency in which they were
conspicuously stronger than the Whigs was the inhabitant boroughs,
which provided the two parties with 27 and 16 seats respectively.
Seven such, Amersham, Callington, Fowey, Minehead, Christchurch,
Warwick and Haverfordwest, were entirely subject to Tory control,
while only 3, King's Lynn, Eye and Lewes, were monopolised by
the Whigs. There was nothing to choose between them in their
share of safe seats in burgage, corporation and freemen boroughs.
Nor, except in the counties, did electorates show a decided preference
for one party or the other, depending on whether they were large or
small. Boroughs with over 500 voters gave the Tories rather more
safe seats than they gave the Whigs – 20 as opposed to 12 – but the
discrepancy was nowhere near as marked as in the counties. The safe
seats were distributed very evenly between the parties in boroughs
with under 500 voters.

The geographical distribution of safe seats indicates more about
the grass roots of Toryism and Whiggism than the type of franchise

or the size of the electorate in the constituencies which harboured them. The Tories were virtually in control of Wales, where they held 14 seats out of a total of 24 throughout the period 1701–15, while the Whigs held only 1. If England is divided into three areas, consisting of fourteen counties in the South and East, thirteen in the South and West, and thirteen in the North, interesting distinctions between the parties begin to emerge. In the South and West, which includes an area bounded by Shropshire, Warwickshire, Oxfordshire, Wiltshire and Hampshire, the Tories could count on 44 borough seats and the Whigs on 27. The further into the West Country one penetrates, the more Tory strongholds are encountered, so that in Cornwall and Devon they had 19 safe seats and their rivals only 3. The Toryism of the 'tipling counties of Devon, Somerset, etc.', as they were then called, was clearly recognised by contemporaries. In a pamphlet written before the 1710 election a Whig lawyer was made to comment adversely on 'the Western Counties, which supply'd us with so many Tackers, and threaten us with so many S[acheverell] lites'.[5] Thus Wales and the West, the bastions of the royalist cause in the civil wars, were the bulwarks of Toryism in the early eighteenth century. The thirteen Northern counties, which stretch as far south as Staffordshire, Leicestershire, Rutland and Lincolnshire, on the other hand, were more evenly balanced in their loyalties. In these counties the Whigs had 16 safe borough seats and the Tories 17, while in one of them, Yorkshire, there were no fewer than 11 safe Whig seats compared with only 2 on the Tory side. The parties were also fairly evenly matched in the South and East, though the Whigs had a slight edge with 24 safe borough seats to 20 for their opponents. However, what is significant is the fact that there were proportionately fewer safe seats in the Home and adjacent counties than in the other areas of the country. Where in Wales 62·5 per cent of all seats were safe, while the share both in the North and South-West of England was 38 per cent, in the South-East it was only 30·7 per cent.

A party gained control of a seat outright either because it was more popular with the electorate than its rival, or because the interest of one or two individuals was so strong in a constituency that it gave them the power of nominating Members. By and large popularity accounted for safe seats in constituencies with electorates of over 500, while patronage secured them in medium and small boroughs.

No individuals had the right of nomination to county seats. The earl of Nottingham, whose seat at Burley on the Hill gave him considerable interest in Rutland, England's smallest county, came nearest to having it during these years. But even he could not single-handedly muster up enough interest to nominate a knight of the shire for Rutland. Although he managed to recommend candidates for one seat successfully throughout the period, it was always in concert with other prominent individuals in the locality. Up to 1710 he co-operated with the Tory interest in the county. When he broke with that party in December 1711 he did not go it alone, but threw in his lot with prominent local Whigs, and it was on the Whig rather than the Finch interest that his son was successful in 1713 and 1715. This is shown by the way the freeholders voted in the elections of 1710 and 1713. At the first Nottingham's son, Lord Finch, stood with Richard Halford against Lord Sherard and John Noel; 236 freeholders gave both their votes to him and Halford, and only 31 gave one vote to him and the other to one of his rivals. By 1713 the situation had been almost exactly reversed. Then Lord Finch stood with Lord Sherard against Halford. This time 218 freeholders gave both their votes to Finch and Sherard, but only 82 of those who voted for Halford also gave one vote to Nottingham's son. These 82 were the hard core of the Finch interest in Rutland, and even this number would have been further reduced if Halford had had a Tory partner in 1713. As it was they could not have returned Lord Finch to Parliament without the addition of the much larger number of votes provided by the Whig adherents of Lord Sherard.

Some of the incumbents of safe seats in large boroughs were nominated by patrons. Thus Lord Exeter's sway over Stamford kept its 2500 electors firm to the Tory interest throughout the period without a contest. In most of these constituencies, however, a contest often revealed how unstable even the most established interests could be. The Hon. James Brydges, for example, represented Hereford for most of the period. In a study of his interest there Professor Godfrey Davies concluded:[6]

Brydges certainly did not nurse his constituency, though his father who lived at the deanery and his many relatives may have kept his name before the freemen. So far as the evidence goes, he held no public meetings and distributed no election literature – no addresses or ballads or caricatures. There is no sign of treating or bribing the general electorate. To cultivate the gentry and city officials, and to canvass for a couple of days, seems to have sufficed to make Hereford a safe seat in eight elections from 1698 to 1713.

This was certainly enough when, as in 1710, no serious opposition offered itself. Two years earlier, however, it had been a very different story. In May 1708 his interest there had been seriously jeopardised, and Brydges took no chances in order to safeguard it.[7] As he explained to the duke of Marlborough:[8] 'popular elections (such as mine consisting of upwards of 1,000 voices) are subject to so many accidents that the strongest family interest is often defeated.'

The point at which patronage became a more important means of controlling seats than popularity cannot be exactly determined. Some boroughs with just under 500 voters were indistinguishable from larger constituencies. The Whigs controlled King's Lynn throughout the period without a contest, apart from one held in the unusual circumstances following the expulsion of Robert Walpole from the Commons in 1712. Yet they were anxious in 1702 at the prospect of a Tory challenge at the polls. As a friend wrote to Walpole, 'where matters depend upon the multitude there must be a great deal of caution used, for they are fickle, easy to be put upon a wrong scent and hard to be reduced again'.[9] On the other hand, proprietary boroughs, where both seats were controlled by a patron, begin to make their appearance in constituencies not much smaller than King's Lynn. Warwick was the largest, where Lord Brooke's interest with the 400 voters could not be moved at four contests. Minehead, with nearly 300, was ruled by the owners of Dunster castle, who kept it firm to the Tory interest. The 120 electors of Morpeth were so dominated by the Whig earl of Carlisle that Sir Edward Blackett was prepared to bet up to £30 that his lordship's nominees would win in 1710, but nobody was prepared to take him on.[10]

Those constituencies with under 100 voters where both seats were held by the same party throughout the period were all proprietary

boroughs. On the Tory side there were ten, exactly twice
as many as the number in the hands of their rivals. Indeed the
Tories had as many small proprietory boroughs in Devon and
Cornwall – Callington, Fowey, Launceston, Saltash and Dartmouth –
as the Whigs had in the rest of the country. At this level were located
the classic 'pocket' boroughs of the unreformed electoral system
Later in the eighteenth century Gatton and Old Sarum were to
become the most notorious examples of this type of constituency.
Gatton was no more independent in Anne's reign than in George III's.
About 1704 Browne Willis visited the borough and was informed by
'Mr Pipps the parson of it . . . that when the writs for members
came down he read it in the church, and that on the day of the
election about 10 or 12 inhabitants meet at the Pound and the
constable takes their votes – Lord Haversham . . . joining with Mr
Turges nominate the parliament men'.[11] Yet as a result of the sale
of its manor in 1704 one seat was transferred from the Whig to the
Tory party at the General Election of 1705. Old Sarum actually
witnessed two contests between 1701 and 1715, and only one of its
seats was retained by the same party, the Tories, throughout those
years. The safest seats in England in the early eighteenth century,
therefore, were located in Beeralston, where the earl of Stamford
owned enough burgages to return two Whigs at every election, and
Newton in Lancashire, whose hundred or so 'votable burgages' were
entirely at the disposal of the Leghs of Lyme, a Tory family.

Most safe seats in fact were not in proprietary boroughs, but in
two-Member constituencies where the other seat fluctuated between
the parties and was often the cause of fierce controversy. This indicates
a marked degree of resistance in this period to the blandishments of
patrons who tried to control a borough's representation outright.
Local magnates might be honoured with the nomination to one seat,
as were the Whig Lord Hervey at Bury St Edmunds and the Tory
earl of Thanet at Appleby. But attempts by them to engross the
other seat were viewed with suspicion. A voter in Appleby complained
in 1701 that 'it was very hard my Lord Thanet should still command
two votes'. Such resistance to the pressure of patronage is further
testimony to the relative independence of the electorate in the early
eighteenth century.

The extent to which patrons could nominate Members during the early eighteenth century can, therefore, be exaggerated. Dr R. Walcott, for example, described some fifty Members of Parliament elected in 1701 as 'nominees'.[12] The term clearly fits a man such as Robert Monckton, who was returned on the duke of Newcastle's interest at Aldborough in Yorkshire. But when knights of the shire are styled 'nominees', the word is being used very dubiously indeed. No individual interest prevailed over county seats in quite the same way as the owner of a pocket borough controlled its representation. Take, for example, Sir William Gostwick, whom Dr Walcott lists as the 'nominee' of the duke of Bedford for one of the Bedfordshire seats. Now powerful though the Russell interest was in that county, it was not all-powerful. In 1705 Gostwick and Lord Edward Russell, the uncle of the second duke of Bedford, were challenged by Sir Pynsent Charnock and John Harvey. Charnock and Gostwick were returned, while Russell and Harvey were unsuccessful. When Sir William held his own while Lord Russell was ousted, it is clear that he was no mere Bedford nominee, but could himself command considerable support in the county.

The limitations of patronage are perhaps best illustrated by the electoral interest of Lord Wharton. Wharton was the most renowned electoral magnate of the period, and his canvassing aroused almost as much comment as his womanising. His prowess in both fields has tended, however, to be exaggerated. Soon after his death an admirer claimed that in 1705 he 'exerted himself so vigorously in all parts of England that it is said he procured the returns of above thirty members for his friends'.[13] His latest biographer asserts that he controlled six seats in Westmorland alone, a truly remarkable feat when one recalls that the county returned only four Members in all.[14] Dr Walcott described eleven Members of the 1701 Parliament as Wharton's 'nominees'. For only four of these, however, was Wharton's support absolutely crucial to their success.[15] The others were returned as much by their own efforts or by the activities of others as by Wharton's influence in their constituencies. One of them, Thomas Lamplugh, actually stood against his interest at Cockermouth.[16]

The number of seats to which patrons could nominate Members

or at least influence their returns was much smaller in this period
than it later became. Sir Lewis Namier calculated that in 1761 205
seats were controlled by the nomination or influence of peers and
commoners.[17] Between 1701 and 1715 the number was nearer 120.

The safest seats in the middle of the century, of course, were at
the disposal of the Ordnance and the Treasury rather than of private
individuals. At the beginning of the century, too, there were some
constituencies in which the Government itself had enough electoral
influence to nominate Members. The postal service at Harwich, the
garrison at Sheerness, the dockyards at Plymouth and Portsmouth, for
example, gave it great influence over local parliamentary seats. Other
governmental agencies also exerted considerable electoral influence.
Thus the Chancellor of the Duchy of Lancaster usually nominated
to one seat at Preston, while the Governor of the Isle of Wight had
a powerful interest on that island. The Cinque Ports, in the words of
a contemporary, were 'much guided by the Lord Warden'.[18]

Such seats were useful for bringing into Parliament placemen with
no strong party affiliations who might not have appealed to local
interests in more partisan constituencies. Thus one of the Cinque
Ports afforded a haven for the politically colourless but administra-
tively indispensable William Lowndes, Secretary of the Treasury
and M.P. for Seaford throughout the period. Not that all Court
nominees in these boroughs were non-party men. The Tory ministry
of 1702 used its interest in the Cinque Ports on behalf of Tories.[19]
When the Whig earl of Westmorland became deputy warden,
therefore, he used the Government's influence on behalf of very
different candidates in the 1705 election, and boasted 'such success
that the members were almost all changed to the principle I was of'.[20]

The Government's interest in these constituencies, however, was
precarious. Members elected on it could not ignore local interests,
as Secretary of State Sir Charles Hedges discovered to his cost in 1701.
He failed to regain his seat at Dover because 'the whole Corporation
is disgusted that since the last election he never came or sent amongst
them to thank them, and that interest on which his last election was
founded is entirely fallen off from him'.[21] Letters sent by M.P.s
to the mayor and jurats of Sandwich show how assiduously they had
to guard their interests there both in and out of Parliament.[22] In 1702

the mayors of Hastings, Sandwich and Winchelsea wrote to their representatives asking them to be present at a case before Queen Anne and the Council concerning the impressing of seamen, a request which was treated as a command.[23] Being a Member on the Government's interest was no automatic way of escaping one's responsibilities to the electorate.

Indeed accommodating local interests went a good deal farther than writing appreciative letters in these constituencies. Often it meant agreeing to share the representation of a borough between a Government and a local candidate. This invariably happened in the three boroughs on the Isle of Wight. It is true that in Yarmouth the local representative, Henry Holmes, also held the post of lieutenant-governor of the island from 1702 to 1706, and again from 1710 to 1714. But since he held a seat in the borough from 1695 to 1717 it would appear that he was given an important local office because of his political influence on the island, and not that he acquired his seat there because of his office.

Dr Walcott, therefore, overestimated the number of seats directly at the disposal of the Government when he described twenty-four constituencies as 'Government Boroughs'.[24] Official interest certainly could not nominate members to anything like the 48 seats in these constituencies. In 1713, for instance, when the Government's interest was used on behalf of the Tories, no fewer than 20 Members returned from them were Whigs. The Government could count on very few men being returned on its own direct interest in this period.

Indeed most reliable Court dependants were chosen without its aid. Though most M.P.s voted consistently Tory or Whig, there were a few who supported the ministry of the day regardless of its party affiliation. Something like 50 or 60 of the 120 or so placemen who sat in any House of Commons at this time could be relied upon to vote for the Court when a division was called.[25] Take a man like the Hon. James Brydges, who sat in the Commons from 1698 until his elevation to the peerage in 1714. Though he was regarded as a Tory at the outset of his career, his tenure of office, first as an Admiralty Councillor and then as Paymaster of the forces abroad, led him to vote with the Government even when it supported Whig measures. His seat at Hereford, therefore, cannot be regarded as a safe seat for either of the two parties. Although he owed it entirely to the interest of his family in the locality it was a seat upon which for all intents and purposes the Government could rely as long as it kept Brydges in office.

There were also some patrons of seats who nominated Court supporters to their boroughs. Thus when Brydges asked Lord Godolphin in 1708 to obtain a seat for him as an insurance against defeat in his own borough, the Lord Treasurer did not scout round for a Treasury seat for him. Instead he approached Hugh Boscawen, a Cornish friend who held the post of Warden of the Stanneries and whose interest with the Corporation of Truro was usually strong enough for him to nominate one of their Members. Boscawen obliged, and Brydges was returned both in Hereford and Truro.[26]

It is important to emphasise that neither of these seats was at the disposal of the Government. They were subject to the influence of individuals who supported the Government, but that was a very different matter. Several boroughs in Cornwall returned placemen to Parliament. But this does not mean that Cornwall was a Court preserve. It merely meant that the Government cultivated the support of Cornish patrons. Jonathan Trelawny, bishop of Exeter until 1707 and thereafter bishop of Winchester, was a prime example of a local territorial magnate who regularly sent up a quiver of courtiers from West Country boroughs. In 1710, however, largely for personal reasons, he put his electoral interest at the disposal of the Whigs.[27]

When Henry St John observed in 1705 that most of the Tackers had sat for safe seats in the previous Parliament, he attributed their security of tenure to the 'prevalency of their party, or the absolute dependancy of their corporations' in the constituencies which they represented.[28] By and large he appears to have been distinguishing between large and small electorates. Counties and boroughs with over 500 voters accounted for 68 safe seats between 1701 and 1715. In most of these the prevalency of one or other of the parties gave gave them electoral control. The remaining 120 seats retained by either the Whigs or the Tories throughout the period were more under the control of electoral proprietors.

Curiously enough, however, the corporation boroughs are exceptions from the general rule that the smaller the electorate was in a constituency then the greater was the likelihood of the seats in it being subject to a rarely contested control. Only Newport in the Isle of Wight was completely controlled, while the others were among the most turbulent and least controllable constituencies of the period. There was a relatively high number of contests in them, only one avoiding a poll between 1701 and 1715, while the contested elections in the remaining seventeen average out at over three in each. There was also a high turnover of seats between the parties in them. Though in some one seat was already under control, as at Bury St Edmunds where Lord Hervey could count on the return of a nominee, over three-quarters of the seats in these constituencies changed sides from Tory to Whig or vice versa at least once in these years. Why even the smallest boroughs could be so politically volatile in the early eighteenth century is the subject of the next chapter.

# CHAPTER SIX

# The Floating Vote

*The lampoons fly as thick as hail in order to influence the approaching elections.*

ERASMUS LEWIS to HENRY DAVENANT,
16 March 1705

*Political instability*

IF in many constituencies the result of any election was a foregone conclusion, in many others the political see-saw elevated the fortunes first of one party and then of the other. Where in 1708 Robert Walpole had correctly predicted that ten of the twelve Norfolk Members would be Whigs, after the 1710 election his Tory uncle Horatio estimated his party's majority in that county to be 'nine out of twelve, where before we had but two'.[1] Other counties, for example Cornwall and Kent, recorded similar huge swings following General Elections held during these years.[2] On the whole there were more frequent fluctuations in the South and East than in the North and West. The party struggle was significantly fiercer in the Home Counties than in the remote provinces, as the relative scarcity of safe seats and higher incidence of contests in them shows.

London and Westminster to some extent set the national trend. Six Members sat for these constituencies, four for London, two for Westminster. After the 1701 election all six were Whigs. In 1702 they returned five Tories and one Whig. At the next election all six Members were again Whigs. Despite the national swing to the Whigs in 1708 the Tories somehow managed to gain three of these seats. In 1710 and 1713 they carried all six, while in 1715 the Whigs regained all but one. Apart from the anomalous returns of 1708, therefore, the political affiliations of the Members returned from

London and Westminster mirrored almost exactly the national trends of the period.

Five counties, Cheshire, Kent, Middlesex, Hampshire and Surrey, also came close to changing their representation in accordance with the prevailing swing at each election. Of these, Cheshire was the only one well away from London. There two Whigs were returned in 1701, 1705 and 1708 and two Tories in 1702, 1710 and 1713, the pattern being broken only in 1715, when one from each party was elected.

Some of the larger boroughs also reflected the ebb and flow of party strength. Derby, Norwich and Coventry, for example, closely followed the moves towards the Tories in 1702, 1710 and 1713, and towards the Whigs in 1701, 1705, 1708 and 1715. Norwich had an electorate of over 3000. Between 1701 and 1715 it was contested on every possible occasion, that is at seven General Elections and one by-election. All these contests were fiercely fought – one of the successful candidates in 1701 scraped home by a single vote. Nor were the disputes confined to parliamentary elections, but raged every year for control of the corporation. In May 1710 'a terrible contest happened there between high church and Whig about the choice of a new mayor, but the first carried it by above 200 votes'.[3] In 1705 the municipal and parliamentary elections actually coincided, and the furore was so violent that Norwich became a byword for 'all the excess of party fury run up to seed. . . . Never was City in this miserable kingdom so wretchedly divided as this. Never were such divisions carried on with such feud, such malice, such magisterial tyranny and such defiance of laws and government.'[4] As the period progressed the violence increased until between the death of Anne and the first General Election of George I's reign the editor of a local Tory paper gave this account of it in a letter to a friend:[5]

> The City of Norwich is at present distracted with party rage, Whig and Tory, High Church and Low Church, or to give it you in our dialect, Croakers and Tackers make the two contending parties. The Whigs here are a strange compound body of false churchmen, Presbyterians, Independents, Anabaptists, Antinomians and Quakers, each of which have Separatists from them, and all conventicles to assemble in. These now think they have

got the ascendant, and threaten destruction to all who jump not
with their Republican notions of Government.

Among the medium-sized boroughs Aylesbury was one whose
representation was fiercely contested in these years, both locally and,
in the case of the Aylesbury men, at national level. Indeed no other
constituency went to the polls more frequently between 1701 and
1715, there being nine contests held there during those years.
Many of these contests were very closely fought, being decided by
only one vote in 1708 and again in 1713. But in 1705 and 1710 the
results were more decisive. In the first of these elections the Whigs
defeated the Tory candidates by a margin of 28 votes, while at the second
the Tories came 36 votes ahead of their rivals. A swing of 64 votes
in a borough with an electorate of about 300 gives some indication
of the violence of the party struggle in this turbulent constituency.

Very few small boroughs followed the national trend closely, for
in these the influence of patronage and money often countered
electoral swings. Freakish though results tended to be, however, there
was nevertheless a significant turnover of Members between the two
parties, even among the smallest constituencies.

The violent see-saw of party fortunes in so many constituencies
reflected the volatility of the early-eighteenth-century electorate.
Ultimately what conditioned a party's parliamentary strength were
the choices made by thousands of individual voters. Why they chose
to side now with the Tories, now with the Whigs, is the key problem
to determine in this chapter.

It could be that electoral behaviour was influenced by thousands
of individual reactions which did not fall into a general pattern.
Contemporaries found it difficult to predict which way voters would
behave. 'Abundance of these country fellows', complained Sir John
Verney of the freeholders in Buckinghamshire, 'stick not to promise
everybody, so that their votes are uncertain until they are in the poll
books.'[6] Even when their votes are known, historians can have
difficulties in interpreting why men voted as they did.

By and large, however, two explanations of voting habits demand
detailed investigation. One is that in casting their votes towards a
certain set of candidates electors had in mind their own self-interest.

Since they expected rewards from their members, not only in immediate bribes but also in the form of posts in the armed forces and in the administration, those candidates fared best who looked like being on the side of the majority in the ensuing Parliament, and therefore in a better position to make available to their constituents the loaves and fishes of Government patronage. Such considerations prompted James Lowther to observe in 1710, 'both parties talk very confidently of a majority, but the times are so corrupt they must know very little that don't think a Court can give either side a majority'.[7]

Another view sees the issues raised by party political propaganda as the key determinant of election results. This does not imply that men worked out their attitude to the political parties rationally then, any more than they do now. It was certainly not a question of the Augustan voter weighing solemnly the merits of the divine right and contract theories of government, or the pros and cons of giving a monopoly of political power to the established Church, or the argument for and against England participating in the War of the Spanish Succession as a principal. Propagandists grossly distorted the nature of the real issues in politics, portraying the Tories as Jacobites, Papists and Francophiles, and the Whigs as Republicans, Presbyterians and Warmongers. As is the case today, propaganda projected the image rather than the reality of party politics. But the stereotypes thus created were readily recognisable by even the illiterate through the media used to get across the message. In so far as they identified now with one, now with the other, so the argument goes, the electors of this period affected the fortunes of the Tory and Whig parties at the polls.

Many contemporaries were convinced that the most important influence on the outcome of elections was exerted by the Government. 'The parties are so near an equality,' the shrewd Lord Cowper advised George I in 1714, with the practice of previous reigns still very fresh in his mind, 'and the generality of the world so much in love with the advantages a king of Great Britain has to bestow, without the least exceeding the bounds of law, that 'tis wholly in your Majesty's power, by showing your favour in due time (before the elections) to one or other of them to give which of them you please a clear majority in all succeeding parliaments.'[8]

As Lord Chancellor, Cowper was well aware of the legal limits of the Crown's electoral influence. He was himself responsible for the issue of the writs calling an election, and, in 1708, when he had previously held the Seals, he had been approached by Lord Wharton to delay the writs for Wiltshire in order to assist the Whig interest in that county.[9] It was through Chancery, too, that the Crown had worked if it wished to tinker with the constitution of a parliamentary borough. The last king to do this on any scale was James II, and he had created an uproar. But the last Lord Chancellor to be accused of interfering with borough charters for political ends was none other than Cowper himself, who in 1707 had put the Great Seal to a new charter for Bewdley in Worcestershire, which gave the Whigs there an advantage over the Tories. This action produced a parliamentary storm. The Bewdley Tories submitted that 'if a corporation may be thus deprived of its right of election, and that right can by charter be transferred to others, all elections in boroughs are ... dependent upon his will to whom the keeping of the Great Seal is committed'. Robert Harley drew up lists of rhetorical questions, asking, *inter alia*, 'whether the Lord of Wingham [Cowper] has not taken more towns by the Great Seal than the lord of Woodstock [Marlborough] will take by storm this campaign', and, even more sinisterly, 'whether the taking away of charters and forcing new ones upon parliament boroughs was one cause of the Revolution'.[10]

But Cowper, one of the finest lord chancellors in English history, was not a sinister man, and the methods which he hinted at in his advice to George I were far removed from those employed by James II. Nor was he advocating the kind of bribery which Walpole resorted to, for it was not until later that significant sums were earmarked from Secret Service funds for the Government's electoral expenses. Between the Revolution and the Hanoverian succession the electoral influence of the Crown was used more subtly than it had been under the absolutist Stuarts or was to be under the oligarchic Whigs. All that Cowper had in mind was the dispensation of the Crown's patronage exclusively to members of the favoured party. In this capacity, too, he was a key figure, for the Lord Chancellor dispensed a great deal of ecclesiastical and judicial patronage.

The Lord Chancellor presented clergymen to livings in the gift of the Crown. These were very often filled with men of the right political persuasion. In 1707 Cowper was approached by Sir John Holland to obtain the living of Banham for a certain Mr Gibbs whose Whig principles Sir John undertook to answer for.[11] When in the same year the Tory archbishop of York asked Cowper to review an appointment which he had just made, he hastened to assure him that 'there is nothing of party in this opposition'.[12] It was his knowledge of the political importance of Church appointments which led Cowper to advise the king 'to use the utmost caution not to prefer any of those ecclesiastics whose known principles lead them to scruple the validity of a limitation of the right to the Crown by Act of Parliament'.[13]

Where the control of ecclesiastical patronage could only be a long-term approach of a Whig Lord Chancellor to the problem of influencing elections, a shorter answer lay in the rigging of the commissions of the peace. Probably never before or since have places on the bench been used on such a scale as part of a political spoils system. The biggest turnover of J.P.s appears to have taken place during the political upheavals of the years 1701–2. In those two years the commissions of the peace were drastically purged in favour first of the Tories, then of the Whigs, and following the death of William III for the benefit again of the Tories.[14] After Anne's accession Sir Edward Seymour was instrumental in ousting twenty-one men from the bench in Devon alone.[15] So great was the transformation at this time that in March 1704 the House of Lords required lists of justices then in commission, and also of those who had been on the bench in 1700, in order, as the Tories supposed, 'to compare 'em and have those turned out restored'.[16] The political rigging of the commissions went on throughout the period. In 1704 the Whig William Fleming was prised off the bench in Westmorland by his Tory colleagues, who reported him to the Cabinet for commenting on the dismissal of the earl of Nottingham from the post of Secretary of State with the words that he 'hoped the Queen now saw the error of employing some men'.[17] The Whigs got their own back when they came to power in 1708. Heneage Finch complained that in Surrey they had put in 'a parcel of scandalous fellows only to act as their rulers direct, and secure an interest by the terror of their power'.[18] There was a reaction in favour of the Tories during the last four years of Anne's reign, but perhaps the biggest purge of all took place in the months after her death, when the Whigs removed their opponents with systematic ruthlessness. Twenty-two justices connected with Robert Harley, including the earl of Oxford himself, were struck off the commission of the peace in Herefordshire shortly after the accession of George I.[19] The new king had taken to heart the advice of Lord Cowper, and shown his favour in due time to the Whigs.

The Crown could also demonstrate its inclinations strikingly by bestowing other offices on members of one party. In particular the posts of lord-lieutenant and sheriff were very influential in county elections.

At the top of provincial society were the lord-lieutenants of the counties. These posts went to the great magnates of the localities, usually to noblemen. They enjoyed considerable patronage as heads of the county militias, and if this was used exclusively on behalf of one party it could tip the balance of power decisively in its favour. When the Whig Earl Rivers replaced the Tory Baron Guilford as lord-lieutenant of Essex in 1705, he took over from his predecessor thirty-one deputy-lieutenants. He deprived sixteen of these officers of their commissions, four of whom were Tory M.P.s who had voted for the Tack in November 1704, and put a further thirteen in their places.[20] In the ensuing General Election the Whigs took both county seats from the Tories. The duke of Beaufort's family interest in Monmouthshire was considerable, quite apart from any official influence he could bring to bear in that county. Yet so crucial did he consider Court patronage to be that he wrote repeatedly to the earl of Oxford in 1713 to urge upon him 'the great loss it will be to the Church interest in Monmouthshire if I am not made lord lieutenant and custos rotulorum of the county'.[21] The Government could give extra weight to a strong local interest by making its head lord-lieutenant, but it could not create a vital influence in this way if there was no natural prestige to build on. 'The lord Peterborough has little or no interest in our country,' Sir Justinian Isham wrote to his son in 1714, 'yet being lord lieutenant 'tis but a compliment he may expect to be asked.'[22]

By contrast the post of sheriff could give the most obscure country

gentleman tremendous influence over county elections, since he acted
as returning officer. There were many things which he could do in
this capacity to assist candidates whom he favoured and to hinder
the elections of those whom he opposed. For instance, he could
advance or retard the date of the election to suit the convenience of
favoured candidates. Thus the high sheriff of Worcestershire assured
Sir John Pakington that he 'need be in no pain touching the time of
our election' in 1705.[23] Sheriffs could arrange for the poll to be
taken at a centre where most of the neighbouring voters were in the
favoured candidates' interest. Gilfrid Lawson complained most
bitterly on this score against the sheriff of Cumberland in 1705:[24]

> I am disappointed in my expectation of a civil and fair treatment
> from the sheriff, who removed his county court to Carlisle, and
> then to Salkeld Yeats, a place upon the edge of this county, which
> you know to be a very large one. For several must come 50 miles,
> and when they come there, can only meet with three or four
> straggling cottages, on the edge of a large moor, no place of accom-
> modation being nearer than Penrith, which is four miles off. . . .
> I could very nigh double Mr Musgrave if the election was in the
> middle of the county, yet can't prevail with the freeholders
> to go so far, and the sheriff has given me such a taste of what
> I must expect, that I shall trouble myself no further on that
> matter.

When polling began, the sheriff could cut short or delay the poll,
whichever would forward the interest of his chosen candidates and
frustrate that of their rivals. Dyer's newsletter accused the sheriff of
Cheshire of holding up the poll five days to weary the Tory gentry
in 1710.[25] Sheriffs could also see to it that the scrutineers of the polls
were biased. The Tory candidates in Essex in 1705 registered an
official complaint to the effect that all the clerks were dissenters.[26]

The job of a sheriff was an irksome and expensive business, which
nobody willingly sought. Anybody who could influence the appointment of a sheriff usually tried to get friends off, and to ensure that
their enemies were chosen. For example, the Whig Lord Shaftesbury
recommended a Tory to be sheriff of Dorset in 1706, while the Tory
Lord Cheyne urged the earl of Oxford to see to it that a Whig
became sheriff of Buckinghamshire in 1714, and to excuse 'a very
honest Tory, not be loaded with that expense of being sheriff if

possibly to be avoided'.[27] Every third year, however, aspiring knights
of the shire would urge one of their friends to accept the office in
order to have a favourable returning officer. Peter Wentworth
reckoned that the Whigs were at an even greater disadvantage due
to the early dissolution of 1710 than they might have been, because
they had directed the Queen's choice 'for sheriffs this year, almost
throughout England of Tories. Their friends they kept off till next
year when they thought they should make use of them in elections
of P—men.'[28]

Just how effective such appointments were it is difficult to judge.
Lord Shaftesbury was convinced that they were vitally important in
helping the Tories to victory in 1702. 'That party whom the Court
has favoured,' he wrote,[29]

> have obtained their victory in almost all parts, by what means or
> practices, lawful or unlawful, moderate or violent I will not say.
> The justices of the peace, the sheriffs, the officers of all the militia
> of all Cities and Counties, with all the rest of the civil and military
> offices were in the hands of the high Church party, and the changes
> reserved to the very instant of the elections, the more to strike a
> terror and break the measures of these who, depending on some
> moderation, had not armed themselves, nor the people they in-
> fluenced, against such an attack on all those that were friends of
> the late Government.

Shaftesbury, however, was on the losing side. A Tory was of a rather
different opinion. Referring to the same election J. Bromley wrote to
Thomas Coke: 'You'll judge by the printed lists how well they go,
and I hope others whom it most concerns will consider what little
help has been given us, and from thence make a right judgement of
the true strength and interest of the kingdom.'[30]

In gauging the weight of the Court's influence in the eighteenth
century it is sometimes claimed that the Government never lost an
election. This might be true of the Hanoverian period, but it is not
strictly correct of this. The ministry which William III hastily
constructed late in 1701 most certainly could not control the House
of Commons elected at the end of that year. But perhaps William's
reign was exceptional. The King's preparations, it could be said,
were always too little, too late and too half-hearted. In Anne's reign

the Government had a much more impressive record of success. In 1702 and 1713 its influence was placed entirely at the service of the Tories, while in 1708 the Whigs benefited from Court support. At all three elections the favoured party won. In 1705 the Court's attempt to prevent either side gaining a working majority met with success, while in 1710, though Harley's dread of a top-heavy Tory majority prevented it being used to full effect, the influence of the Crown was clearly on the side of the Tories, who emerged victorious. However, on all these occasions public opinion was also on the winning side, which makes it impossible to calculate the extent to which government support assisted it. It would have been fascinating for the historian if Queen Anne had broken with the Tories in 1711, gone over to the Whigs, and dissolved Parliament. Two contemporaries gave Baron Robethon their opinion of the likeliest outcome of such an intriguing chain of events in March of that year.[31] Lord Townshend was 'convinced that, provided the Queen made as much interest for the Whigs in the ensuing elections as she had previously done for the Tories, then they would certainly have the majority'. The duke of Marlborough was 'of a different opinion. He said that since the existing parliament had done nothing outrageous enough to open the eyes of the people, who were seduced by the clergy, they would run the risk of the new parliament being even worse than the present one, whatever efforts the Queen might make in favour of the Whigs.'

While many contemporaries attributed electoral gains and losses to the influence of the Court, others besides Marlborough saw them as the outcome of changes in public opinion. Thus the judicious Lord Somers, drawing up 'Heads of Arguments' to induce King William to call a new Parliament in 1701, placed at the very top of his list 'the present ferment and disposition of the nation'.[32] In 1708 Joseph Addison informed the earl of Manchester, 'it is believed this intended invasion will have a great influence on the elections for the ensuing parliament'.[33] Where the Pretender's abortive landing was held to have helped the Whigs in 1708, two years later Sacheverell's prosecution was regarded as having turned opinion in favour of the Tories to such an extent that James Craggs prophesied, 'I will be bold to

D

foresee as the common people are now set they will get at least three for one. . . .'[34]

The Government itself acknowledged the importance of public opinion by appealing to it when Parliament was dissolved. In 1701 the Proclamation announcing the dissolution was a thinly disguised appeal to the electorate to return Whig candidates:[35]

> Whereas our loving subjects have universally, by their loyal addresses, expressed their resentment of the injustice and indignity offered to us, and our people, by the late proceedings of the French king, in taking upon him to own and declare the pretended Prince of Wales to be king of England . . . We have received the same with great satisfaction, and have thought it reasonable, in this extraordinary juncture, to give our subjects the opportunity of choosing such persons to represent them in Parliament, as they may judge most likely to bring to effect their just and pious purposes.

Queen Anne did not issue similarly provocative proclamations, but she did make her views felt in her speeches upon the dissolution of Parliament. Her assertion in 1713 that she was in perfect accord with the house of Hanover was held to have aided the Tories considerably in their election campaigns.[36] At the end of the period George I reverted to propaganda by proclamation, and the one with which he dissolved Parliament in 1715 was flagrantly partisan, urging the electorate to have 'a particular regard to such as shewed a firmness to the Protestant succession when it was most in danger'.[37]

Each General Election held in this period was fought over great issues. In 1701 the Whigs clamoured for war with France, while the Tories deplored the snap dissolution. At the next election the Tories hailed Anne's accession as a timely remedy for all the ills which they alleged the Revolution had brought with it, and the Whigs sought to preserve the memory of William as the saviour of English liberties. In 1705 the Church provided the most burning issue, the Tories claiming that it was in great danger, the Whigs accusing the Tories of being virtual traitors for having voted for or sympathised with the Tack. The Pretender's attempted invasion was the main subject of electoral publicity in 1708, while in 1710 the impeachment of Dr Sacheverell and the subsequent ministerial revolution produced whole libraries of party propaganda. At the last election held under Anne the parties went to the polls arguing the merits of the Peace of Utrecht and the commercial treaty with France. Finally in 1715 the Whigs harped on the theme of the Succession, while the Tories tried once more to raise the old battle cry 'the Church in danger'.

These were the main issues which employed the energies of party propagandists at elections held between 1701 and 1715. Besides them there were any number of relatively minor questions, such as the impeachments in 1701; the affair of the Aylesbury men in 1705; the debate over the abortive peace negotiations at The Hague, the naturalisation of foreign Protestants and the immigration of the Palatines in 1710; and the failure to destroy the fortifications of Dunkirk in 1713.

Each party employed a great variety of methods to exploit every issue, both permanent and passing, to produce the maximum advantage for itself and the maximum disadvantage for its rival. In particular they made use of two media of mass communication, the pulpit and the Press. Of these the first was probably the more persuasive, since it had nation-wide coverage and reached even the illiterate, though there was a provincial Press and the London periodicals and pamphlets circulated far beyond the capital.

Among the religious bodies in England under Queen Anne the established Church was not only by far the largest, but also the most politically active. Most Members of Parliament were Anglicans, Roman Catholics being debarred by the Test Act of 1678 from taking seats in either House, while very few dissenters sat in the Commons. Of the dissenting congregations only the Quakers had developed an effective extra-parliamentary pressure-group. Under William they campaigned for the legal recognition of their marriage services and for exemption from the payment of tithes.[38] In Anne's reign this agitation was sustained, and in the 1705 election the Quakers sent circular letters to Friends throughout the country directing them to vote for candidates who would sympathise with these aims.[39] Most dissenters, along with the Roman Catholics, probably felt that their interests were best served by keeping quiet. The nearest they got to running a campaign in these years was to agitate during the parliamentary session of 1708–9 for the repeal of the first Test Act so far as it affected themselves. This agitation alarmed the Tories, but came to an abrupt end on 12 January 1709 when the House of Commons passed without opposition a motion to burn a pamphlet advocating the repeal.[40]

When the news reached Devon that the pamphlet had been burned, if Dyer is to be believed, *Te Deum* was sung in Exeter Cathedral.[41] This was one way in which the Church of England reacted to political events in Anne's reign. A more conventional and less controversial method was to ring the bells, a practice which greeted any national news which redounded to the benefit of the Church, and which brought important events to the attention of those within earshot of the belltowers of parish churches throughout England. Those who attended services were often subjected to harangues about politics from the pulpit. Political sermons were the order of the day, whether delivered before Queen and Parliament assembled in St Paul's or read to the humble congregation of some remote parish. All manner of occasions provided opportunities for such sermons, from thanksgiving days for such memorable events as Marlborough's famous victories and the Union with Scotland, to a by-election in a remote constituency. One of the most famous sermons in English history was preached before the City fathers on 5 November 1709 by Dr Sacheverell. His high-flying rant against 'false brethren' in high places would be echoed in parish churches throughout the land.

The 'Tory Roryism' of the lower clergy meant that sermons enjoining the faithful to vote for the Church party were frequently delivered on behalf of Tory candidates in both municipal and parliamentary elections. Sir Gilbert Heathcote's bid for the mayoralty of London in 1710 was opposed by the parson who preached the election sermon, though the implications of divine displeasure failed to prevent the Whig banker from obtaining a great majority.[42] The Church interest was more successful in the parliamentary election at Durham in 1708 where[43]

> By the order of the Bishop and Chapter, as supposed, the School master . . . preached before them at the Cathedral in the morning, and the same sermon in the afternoon to the Mayor and Aldermen at the market place church. The text was the verse [*sic*] of the 12th chapter of the 1st of Samuel, and the words, they say, by

hard straining he perverted into the management of elections, on which his whole discourse run, lashing all those who opposed Mr Conyers, concluding that damnation would be their future lot, if they did not repent of such an heinous sin as the attempting to reject so true and trusty a member of the Church.

Conyers and his Tory colleague were duly elected, though their success probably owed more to the fact that the Whig candidate declined to poll than to any fears the voters might have had for their immortal souls. Politics and perdition were even more directly linked by 'a certain parson in Hertfordshire', who, according to a report of the 1705 election in Tutchin's rabidly Whig *Observator*, 'out of his passionate zeal for High-Church said "The Devil take me, if it be not a greater sin to poll against the Tackers than to murder my own father"'.44

Where most sermons were delivered in favour of Tory candidates, Bishop Lloyd of Worcester put on the whole armour of Whiggery to oppose Sir John Pakington, who stood as a candidate for the county in July 1702. Lloyd chose the month of the election to go on a visitation of his diocese. In his opening sermon 'he told his audience . . . without naming him but so plainly that every one must understand who he meant, that he was so debauched and occasioned so much drunkenness in the county he was very unfit to be their representative, and at the same time recommended his concurrents as very fit'.45 'In his visitation sermon at Evesham he complained grievously of the danger we are lately fallen into, of Popery and in greater than in any time of late years', a Pakington supporter informed Lord Hatton, adding later, 'The good Bishop charges his clergy in his visitation everywhere upon their canonical obedience not to give their votes for Sir J. Pak: one of them told him they thought that went not to civil matters and that he believed himself tied as much or more in this to go along with his patron. . . . He told them that to give Sir John their vote was to thrust a dagger in his throat.'46 Lloyd's over-enthusiastic advocacy of the Whig cause did him no good at all. 'The Bishop,' wrote a hostile Tory clergyman, 'with all his blackening aspersions, was so far from prejudicing his [Pakington's] cause, or hindering his election, that he lost ground by the violence of his heat. For he could not so much as influence the clergy of his own collation, or the tenants that held land by lease from him, or the church, to vote against Sir John Pakington.'[47] Not only was Sir John elected, but Lloyd earned a parliamentary rebuke and the loss of his office as almoner to the Queen.

To supplement their oratory the clergy frequently employed the Press. In Crediton Defoe came across a congregation in 1705 which every Sunday devoutly resorted to what its members called a 'news-house' to hear the latest news before going into church.[48] Robert Harley was told in 1710 of a parson in Scarborough who regularly received the *Examiner*: 'it comes hither on Sunday and after evening service the parson usually invites a good number of his friends to his house, where he first reads over the paper, and then comments upon the text, and all the week after carries it about with him to read to such of his parishioners as are weak in the faith, and have not yet the eyes of their understanding opened; so that it is not doubted but he will in time make as many converts to the true interest of the State, as ever he did to the Church'.[49] Not content with making use of the printed products of other pens, some prominent clergymen had their sermons published. It was generally reckoned that about 40,000 copies of Sacheverell's famous sermon were printed and dispersed throughout the nation.

In its printed form Sacheverell's sermon, though it might have been a best-seller, was but one of countless pamphlets which flowed from the Press in this period. Some of those which caused the most stir were written by the finest writers of the Augustan age – Daniel Defoe's *Shortest way with the Dissenters*, Jonathan Swift's *The Conduct of the Allies* and Richard Steele's *The Crisis*, for example. Politicians recognised the formidable power of their pens and were anxious to harness it for their purposes. Thus Robert Harley employed Swift, Defoe and Charles Davenant. Nor did he merely hire propagandists, but himself composed the occasional tract. Other politicians also used the Press to publicise their views. Lord Rochester, son of the first earl of Clarendon, expounded his Tory philosophy in the prefaces to the first edition of his father's *History of the Great Rebellion*. Lord Haversham regularly published his annual perorations to the peers on the state of the nation, while speeches made by members in the Commons were often printed and sold. The fiercest Press campaign of the reign was launched in 1713 over the merits of the peace in general and the commercial treaty with France in particular.

This spate of propaganda became a flood at election times. In 1708 it was reported that printed advices to the voters had been distributed to every constituency,[50] while in 1713 the mayors of many corporations received letters asking them to declare for the Pretender, which was doubtless an unscrupulous Whig trick to smear their opponents with the charge of Jacobitism.[51] Another form of electoral propaganda was the black list, showing individual constituencies how their representatives had voted on controversial issues in the previous Parliament. Almost all of those eventually published in *A Collection of White and Black lists, or a view of those gentlemen who have given their votes in parliament for and against the Protestant religion and succession . . . ever since the Glorious Revolution to the happy accession of king George,* which appeared in 1715, had started life as election tracts. A list of Tories alleged by the Whigs to be friends of France was circulated round Coventry in 1701.[52] Another, listing alleged Tackers, was taken about Queenborough by a Whig agent in 1705, with dire consequences for himself.[53] 'The printing of the commerce bill and the list of members *pro* and *con* has done the Tories no service', Henry Newman observed in August 1713, 'and yet Abel [Roper] has innocently published it in his last *Post Boy*.'[54]

Newspapers were particularly serviceable to party politicians. On 11 March 1702 the *Daily Courant*, London's first daily paper, made its debut. In the middle years of Anne's reign some 44,000 newspapers were sold each week, while by 1712 the figure had risen to about 67,000.[55] In 1705 at least twelve printed newspapers were in circulation,[56] many of them being organs of party opinion. Among the more extreme were John Tutchin's Whig *Observator* and Charles Lesly's Tory *Rehearsal*. Almost as partisan was Dyer's bi-weekly newsletter, which was written with a fanatical High-Church Tory bias. His observations on the election of 1705 were so scandalous that his opponents printed extracts from them in order to expose him.[57] Dyer was a great favourite with Tory country gentlemen, who loved the political slant which he gave to the news. The original newsletters were in manuscript, Dyer employing clerks for the purpose of copying them. Even so it was produced in large numbers and enjoyed a wide circulation. William Bowes found it 'very common in these northern parts' when he wrote to John Ellis from Durham in May 1705.[58] Addison ridiculed its rustic popularity in his caricature of the country gentleman published in the *Freeholder* in 1715: '"Sir," says he, "I make it a rule never to believe any of your printed news. We never see, Sir, how things go, except now and then in Dyer's letter, and I read that more for the stile than the news. The man has a clever pen it must be owned."'[59] Addison's sarcasm becomes more apparent when it is recalled that the greatest writers of the age participated in the production of periodicals, Addison himself contributing to the *Spectator* along with Steele, Defoe producing the *Review*, Swift writing for the *Examiner*. These were merely the brightest stars in a whole galaxy of journalists which made this a golden age for Grub Street.

Since the advent of radio, television and the cinema another form of sustaining mass interest in politics, namely the popularisation of political ballads, songs and poems, has given way to these more sophisticated media, at least in England. But before technology had developed these methods of communication, and education had prepared society to receive them, the simple jingle or doggerel chant was about the only way of putting across political arguments to every section of the population. How potent a force this could be in the late seventeenth century can be seen from the success of Wharton's ballad 'Lillibullero' during the period of the Revolution, which, its author later boasted, had whistled a king out of three kingdoms! Nothing quite so popular fired the imagination under William and Anne, though not for want of material. Indeed their reigns produced any amount of ballads, songs and catches, some even to the memorable tune of 'Lillibullero', though that of 'Chevy Chase' seems to have been more popular.[60] The Sacheverell affair in particular inspired composers and rhymesters, but judging by the quality of their productions this genre produced nothing like the same amount of talent as journalism did in the same period.

Pulpit, Press and ballads disseminated events and opinions throughout the land and were the most effective means of influencing national opinion, but they did not exhaust the repertoire of the political propagandist. There were other means of persuasion at his disposal, for example public spectacles. These were obviously limited in their direct appeal, but if they were staged in London they could command considerable attention, since the eyes of the nation were fixed on the capital, and very often what London did one day the provinces did the next. This was held to be particularly true of parliamentary elections, and the party organisers stage-managed their campaigns to capture control of the City very carefully, since they agreed that it 'generally has a great influence upon other elections'.[61] The Whigs had a particular flair for the theatrical, in the most literal sense, for the leading dramatists of the age – Addison, Congreve, Farquhar and Vanbrugh – were all of that party. This ensured that the London season was dominated by Whig-inclined plays at a time when audiences liked the theatre to be politically committed.[62] The Whigs contributed more materially to the stage when they raised subscriptions through the Kit-Cat Club for the building of the Haymarket Theatre, which opened its doors to the public on 9 April 1705.[63] In 1709, when times generally were bad and opinion was running against the Whigs, Lord Halifax drew up a paper for 'a subscription of four hundred guineas for the encouragement of good comedies'[64] – presumably to lighten the gloom. This sense of the theatrical was projected by the Whigs onto a national stage. Thus they gave maximum publicity to the Sacheverell trial by staging it in Westminster Hall, ultimately to their own discomfort. In 1711 they even tried to revive the Pope-burning processions which had been lively features in the political campaigns of the first Whigs during the Exclusion crisis.[65] A midnight procession was planned for 17 November, the anniversary of Queen Elizabeth's accession, in which effigies of the Devil (made to resemble Robert Harley!), the Pope, some cardinals and Dr Sacheverell were to be burned. Unfortunately for the Whigs, who were reported as having laid out one thousand pounds in preparation for the spectacle, it was suppressed by the authorities.[66]

The Tories do not seem to have had quite the same organising genius for staging public spectacles as the Whigs, though they did not altogether fail to take advantage of the opportunities which presented themselves. During Sacheverell's trial London mobs attacked dissenting chapels and threatened even the Bank. The irony of the situation was not lost on one dyed-in-the-wool Tory observer, who commented, 'we are now come to fresh paradoxical circumstances, that while the rabble are pulling down houses out of zeal for passive obedience the vile tools of the most arbitrary ministry that ever nation groaned under are rending their throats in defence of forcible resistance'.[67] Burnet, who was an eye-witness of these events, was convinced that 'there was a secret management in this matter'.[68] Though the London demonstrations were almost certainly impromptu, the Tories did organise an elaborate progress for their hero from the capital to his new living at Selattyn in Shropshire, which was offered to him by a Tory M.P.[69]

> About the middle of May, Dr Sacheverell went from London to Oxford, where he arrived with a numerous attendance; and was welcomed, and magnificently entertained by the Earl of Abingdon, Mr Charles Bertie, Fellow of All Souls, Mr Rowney, one of the members of Parliament for that city, the Vice-Chancellor, the Heads of Houses, and most persons of distinction in that University. Here he continued the remainder of that month, and on Thursday, the 1st of June, set out from thence for Shropshire, under pretence of taking possession of a living lately bestowed upon him in that county, by Mr Lloyd; but, as was the general opinion, with no other design, than to make himself still more popular, and to confirm the People in the High-Church Interest, in case, as they expected, the Queen should dissolve the Parliament.

Along his route he was entertained by the clergy and gentry, and the bells of nearly every parish church were rung in greeting, except where Whig magistrates had ordered the clappers to be removed.[70]

The effectiveness of such propaganda campaigns varied from constituency to constituency. By and large they had most impact in the counties and larger boroughs, though their influence was also felt in many smaller boroughs.

The counties were particularly sensitive gauges of opinion. 'It is agreed', remarked Swift, 'that the truest way of judging the disposition of the people, in the choice of their representatives, is by computing the county elections.'[71] Thomas Coke's supporters in Derbyshire were very alarmed early in 1704 at a rumour that he had voted against the Occasional Conformity Bill, which if not denied would jeopardise his interest among the Tory gentry. One of them informed him: 'Mr Spateman in all companies boasted of the thing, and drunk your health, saying he would never vote against you for the future. This sort of discourse gave a mighty shock to your friends, who speak of it to me with great concern. I think two words from yourself that I might show them would effectually justify you.'[72] 'It is impossible to imagine what an influence the crying the Church is in danger has among the vulgar in this country', complained a Shropshire Whig in 1710. 'When any of the high Church begs a vote for themselves or party the question they ask the freeholders is if he be not for the church, then if he answers yes, then be for us.'[73] In Kent at the same election an onlooker observed that 'the proceedings against Dr Sacheverell have convinced a great number of men that no good was intended to the Church'.[74] The Sacheverell virus even infected so remote a region as Wensleydale in Yorkshire. An agent of the Tory candidate Sir Arthur Kay found that at Middleham 'all the town are Sacheverellians and value themselves mightily upon it'.[75]

The larger boroughs, too, acted as weathercocks of public opinion. Two in particular, as we have seen, were regarded as pointers towards the prevailing current – London and Westminster. Of these Lord Halifax observed in 1705: 'the countrys always take the rule from hence, and the true pulse of a nation is always felt at the heart'.[76] Because of this the Court usually tried to stage-manage the elections in the capital in order to influence opinion. But the seven thousand or so who voted in the City could not easily be manipulated. When the Whigs carried all four seats in 1705 Halifax commented: 'this change comes naturally, without any force or art. The magistracy and lieutenancy of the City are still in the hands in which my Lord Nottingham placed them, and yet his creatures can make no more of it.'[77]

Public opinion also made itself felt in a medium-sized borough such as Abingdon, where there were about 500 voters. Abingdon was a single-member constituency. The near-by estates of Sir Simon Harcourt at Stanton Harcourt and Nuneham Courtenay conferred upon him an interest in that borough which a little judicious management with the corporation, of which he had himself made recorder, was normally sufficient to convert into effective control. Twice, however, in Anne's reign Sir Simon encountered abnormal conditions.

In 1708 he was unseated on a petition being presented to Parliament by a rival Whig candidate, which most observers regarded as an example of scandalous injustice from a highly partial majority in the House of Commons. Three years earlier, however, he had been defeated by thirty-five votes in a contest with Grey Neville.[78] Though Harcourt himself petitioned, doubtless expecting as Solicitor-General to receive a sympathetic hearing from the Committee of Privileges and Elections, as close a friend as Henry St John was quite satisfied that he had been fairly beaten. 'Harcourt's [election] I could not influence', he wrote to Robert Harley shortly after Sir Simon's defeat, 'and there is so much merit in being against the Tack, whatever some wise men may think, that Nevil was not to be opposed.'[79] The religious issue in a town which was 'full of dissenters' had been enough to turn the scales.[80]

Even in the narrow constituencies there are signs that issues could sway the electors. For instance, Lord Bruce, whose electoral interest in Wiltshire operated in some of the most venal boroughs in England, found that his influence there was adversely affected in 1710 by a report put about by his adversaries that he had voted against Dr Sacheverell.

Political issues, then, played a major role in contested elections in this period. One indication of this is the incidence of contests. So far from following the long-term trend towards fewer contests the tendency in the early eighteenth century was in the opposite direction. Starting with between eighty and ninety at the first two elections of our period they rose to over a hundred in 1705. After falling just below a hundred again in 1708 there was another steep rise in 1710 to about 130, a record for these years, and a number which indicates the extraordinary nature of that election. Although in 1713 the total fell again into the nineties, the movement was reversed eighteen months later when something like 110 constituencies went to the polls at the first General Election to take place under the Hanoverians.

One of the main reasons for the political turbulence of these years was that the electorate felt itself to be involved in the momentous issues which were dividing the political nation. It is no coincidence that the highest number of contests occurred in 1705, 1710 and 1715, years when 'the Church in danger' was the chief political slogan.

The passion engendered by religious disputes was the most explosive electoral ingredient of the period.

Later in the eighteenth century, when political issues were no longer so fundamental and when the political nation was largely united into one governing class, the electorate became apathetic. Since the vote no longer mattered it was worth selling to the highest bidder. In the mid-eighteenth century, as a modern historian has put it, 'the electorate . . . based their choice on local and personal, and seldom on national, issues'.[81]

Things were very different between 1701 and 1715. As a contemporary observed:[82]

> What chiefly inclines the electors, in the preference of the persons to represent them, is the opinion they have of the good dispositions of such persons to serve them and their country by voting and speaking for their nation's good. This, their good opinion of men, will arise in different persons from very different reasons: in some in that they, by themselves or friends, receive some advantages or favours, or have some dependence in point of interest upon them whom they elect. But the most popular reason, and so of greatest use in the counties, cities and great boroughs, where the right of election is in the populace, is an opinion that the persons elected will endeavour the security of the religion they profess and the properties they enjoy. And for this reason men that differ in religion and interest so often disagree about the persons they would elect.

# CHAPTER SEVEN

# The General Election of 1705

> *By the last post the account of the elections stood thus. There*
> *were 385 members chosen; of these 125 are new, and 32*
> *Tackers are turned out.*
>
> HENRY ST JOHN to the<br>DUKE OF MARLBOROUGH, 25 May 1705

THE General Election of 1705 affords the best opportunity of the period for studying the relative effectiveness of Government influence and party propaganda at the polls. This is because in the election campaign of that year the aims of the Government and of the propagandists were more distinct than on any other occasion, and can therefore be more readily examined independently.

Electoral strategy in 1705 was shaped by the historic decision of 134 Tories to tack the Occasional Conformity Bill to the Land Tax Bill in November 1704. This desperate measure, prompted by two previous failures to get the Bill passed by the House of Lords, deeply divided the Tory party. Over one hundred Tories either abstained from voting, thereby being derided as 'Sneakers', or even voted against the Tack. This split lasted for the rest of the parliamentary session.

The Government's campaign was designed to perpetuate this division in the hope that moderate Tories, as distinct from the Tackers, would continue to support the ministry in the new Parliament, thereby making the ministers less dependent upon the Whigs. All ministerial efforts were therefore devoted to keeping out of Parliament any Tories who had voted for the Tack, but to doing nothing which would impede the return of moderate Tories. Government publications, led by Defoe's *Review*, preached the virtues of moderation.

Whig propagandists, on the other hand, made little of these distinctions. On the contrary, they misrepresented the Tack, and implicated the whole Tory party in the project. They argued that the Tackers really designed to assist Louis XIV and the Pretender. Thus one lampoon imagined the French King saying:

> Tho *Malbro'* has ruin'd my Cause
> I'll soon that matter restore,
> For amongst the Makers of Laws
>     I've 130 and 4.

> The Cub that I've cherish'd so long,
> In time will pay off his score,
> For I find his Party is strong,
>     'Tis 130 and 4.

> I'll send him home to his Throne,
> Which his Father abandon'd before,
> I'm sure he will be maintain'd,
>     By the 130 and 4.

Whig attacks were not merely directed against the 134, but branded all Tories, even Sneakers, as being the same way inclined. For instance, the two sneaking knights of the shire for Northamptonshire were lampooned by their Whig opponents in the following verse:[1]

> Here's a Health to the *Knight*
> Who dares *Vote* and dares *Fight*
> To maintain our Religion and Laws, Sir,
>     Against *France* and the *Tack*,
>     And every mad *Jack;*
> And never will *Sneak* from the Cause, Sir.

Some Whigs accused the whole Tory party of sympathising with the Tack, and therefore of being prepared to wreck a major money Bill and to imperil the war effort in order to force their pet Bill onto the statute-book.

Under these attacks the Tory ranks closed. Their writers excused the Tack as being at worst an excess of zeal on the part of devoted Anglicans, and at best as the badge of loyalty to Queen and Church.

The cry 'the Church in danger' was raised, and although the arguments behind the slogan received their most notorious exposition only after the election, in *The Memorial of the Church of England*, the sentiments which that libel expressed were current in Tory circles during the weeks that preceded its publication in July 1705. Just as the Whigs drew few distinctions between Tackers and Sneakers, so the Tories failed to distinguish between the Government and the Whigs, but depicted both as being in league with dissenters to ruin the Church.

There were therefore two separate election campaigns in the spring of 1705. One, sponsored by the Government, was aimed at keeping up the divisions in the Tory party and at retaining the moderates on the side of the ministry. The other, waged by the parties themselves, sought to minimise divisions and to close ranks. The effectiveness of these campaigns can be illustrated by following their progress from start to finish.

The Government began its campaign against the Tackers by dismissing those who held offices under the Crown. Eleven of them had in fact been in official posts, eight of whom were sacked before the General Election, including the Governor of Sheerness, who had electoral influence at Queenborough, and the Governor of Chester Castle. Every effort was made to ensure that no sign could be interpreted as favouring the Tacking cause. The two placemen who were left in – General Charles Seymour and Colonel William Seymour – were spared, it was said, only because they had been forced to vote for the Tack by their father, Sir Edward Seymour.[2] The Court even held over the call of serjeants-at-law because two Tackers appeared on the list.[3]

Another move was to alter the lord-lieutenants of six counties whose Members had been Tackers – Cheshire, Cornwall, Essex, Kent, Oxfordshire and Suffolk. Altogether twenty-nine knights of the shire had voted for the Tack, but the lieutenancies of other counties with Tacking Members were left untouched, presumably because the Government considered them to be in safe hands.

Besides such routine matters more positive steps were taken to announce the ministry's intentions to the electorate. The main public platform for this revelation was the University of Cambridge, one of the Members for which, Arthur Annesley, had in the previous Parliament supported the Tack. The ground was well prepared. In mid-April the Queen herself honoured the university with an official visit. At a ceremony held there on 16 April sixteen peers, including the earls of Sunderland and Orford, and Lord Wharton, and five commoners were made honorary Doctors in Law. All the peers were Whig, some extremely so, while none of the commoners were in the Tacking interest, except, rather surprisingly, Sir Thomas Hanmer. That done, the Queen knighted John Ellis, James Montague and Isaac Newton. If Hanmer's role in the ceremony gave the Tackers any cause for joy, this would have been dashed by the memory that Montague had been imprisoned by order of the Tory House of Commons during the previous Parliament for acting on behalf of the Aylesbury men, and by the knowledge that Newton was to be one of the official candidates intended to remove Annesley.[4] The other was Godolphin's son, Francis, Lord Rialton.

How far the Government was prepared to go in its campaign against the Tackers is indicated by a memorandum of Secretary of State Robert Harley, who, some time before the elections took place, anticipated their probable outcome in a great many constituencies.[5] His predictions are a fascinating insight into the resources at the disposal of the ministry, and of their limitations. He had drawn up a list of constituencies in every county in England and Wales, along-side which were written notes. Some of these jottings are quite full: e.g. 'Lincolnshire: Sir John Thorold. q. Ellis + Ld Chamberlain if the champion could be persuaded.' Most of them, however, are very succinct: e.g. 'Cornwall — Ld Tr.'

*In toto* the information added up to a wealth of detail about the circumstances obtaining in counties and boroughs throughout the realm, and is a tribute to the efficient intelligence service which the Secretary commanded. The use to which he put this knowledge is not easy to determine in view of the cryptic nature of the notes. The short entries merely state who had the interest in a certain area or a particular constituency. Lord Treasurer Godolphin, who re-placed Lord Granville as lord-lieutenant of Cornwall, was, apparently, to foster the Government's interest in that county, while against Newton, Isle of Wight, appears the precise sentence, 'Worseley has the interest'. The fuller notes, however, appear to indicate the Government's aims in certain constituencies. In Lincolnshire Sir John Thorold, a Tacker, was presumably to be kept out with the help of the marquis of Lindsey, who was both lord-lieutenant of the county and also Lord High Chamberlain. At this early stage Harley seems to have been uncertain as to the feasibility of opposing the other Tacking knight of that shire, Lewis Dymoke, the Champion of England. In the event two candidates were set up against Thorold and Dymoke. Against Bury St Edmunds, which had returned the Tacker Sir Robert Davers at the previous election, Harley wrote, 'dispute — Ld Hervey to be set up'.

The Government, therefore, left few stones unturned when making its preparations. Once they were completed there was little left to do but await the results.

The main election campaign began when the Proclamation summoning a new Parliament was published in the *Gazette* for 23–26 April. On 2 May the Lord Keeper sent out writs to the returning officers, and the first three results – Amersham, Malden and Hertford – were announced on 7 May. High-Church Tories jubilantly claimed all three as victories. 'We have an account that these Elections were made yesterday,' wrote Dyer in his newsletter for 8 May,[6] 'viz. Malden in Essex, Will. Fytche and Joh. Comyns Esquires, Tackers: Town of Hertford, Charles Caesar and Rich Gulston Esquires, Tackers: Agmondesham, Lord Cheyne and Sir Sam. Garrard, Bar, the last a Tacker, the other a Well-wisher to them; so that there's five out of six, which is a good beginning, and it's believed very few of the 134 will miss of their elections, notwithstanding the senseless clamours of Whiggish Libellers.'

The jubilation with which Tory papers greeted these early results was, however, premature. As Lord Halifax informed the duchess of Marlborough a few days later[7]

Great care was taken to publish in the 'Flying Post' of Wednesday that the old members were sure again for Malden, Hertford and Amersham, five of which were Tackers. This made a great noise at first with those that were ignorant of the circumstances of those elections, and had an appearance that the Parliament would be much the same. But there was really nothing in it, for as to

Malden nobody stood, or can pretend to stand till the humour is much altered in Essex, for they have made all the parsons and creatures of the bishop of London free of the town. At Amersham Sir Tho Webster carried it by 27 votes, though the officer will return Ld Cheyne and Sir Sam Garret and Sr Tho must be left to petition. At Hertford Mr Clarke has good grounds to petition. . . . But in the other elections we have already turned out six or seven, and brought in as many.

Halifax proceeded to instance Whig successes at Abingdon, Wallingford, Aylesbury, Wendover, Colchester, Rochester, Guildford and Southwark. Before the election these constituencies had been represented by ten Tories and five Whigs. After it they returned to Parliament fourteen Whigs and one Tory. Even Dyer had to admit these as reverses, and on 10 May lamented, 'We have an account of a pretty many elections since my last, but Fortune has favoured the wrong side.' He did, however, attempt to cheer up his readers by informing them that a Tacker had been successful at St Albans, despite the personal intervention of the duchess of Marlborough against him, and by reporting that the Tacking members for Oxford-shire, Oxford and Oxford University had been returned again. Whereas the news of the St Albans success would warm the cockles of High-Church hearts, the results from Oxfordshire can only have given them cold comfort. In the first place the only real attack on their interest took place in Oxford itself. The county was uncontested, while the university witnessed one of the more bizarre contests of the election, in which three Tackers fought for the honour of its representation. In the second place Oxfordshire was the very bastion of the cause, all nine of its members having voted for the Tack. This gave rise to a scurrilous verse, 'The Oxfordshire Nine':

> Perusing the List of the Tackers in Print,
> And carefully marking what Members were in't,
> Some Names I observed to most counties did fall:
> But *Oxford* afforded no fewer than All . . .

Had the Whigs carried Oxford the heart of the High-Church citadel would have fallen. As it was the Whigs put up a much better showing there than they had done in 1701, when they had last contested the city. Then their candidates could raise only 112 votes between them, against 966 cast for the Tories. Now they picked up 350 votes, though the Tory poll was higher than at the previous contest, totalling 1150.

There was even colder comfort for the Tories in the results announced during the rest of the first week of the election. 'The elections go on yet as I wish', Lord Halifax wrote to the duchess of Marlborough on 12 May,

> and there has not been one Whig turned out but in Suffolk and at Gatton in Surrey. For the first your Grace has heard enough, and the other was depending in a manor which honest lord Haversham has sold to a Tory. There is no great alteration in the members that are mentioned in the newspapers today, but some we have, and those are all on our side. Sir Thomas Littleton has thrown out Miller at Chichester. The duke of Richmond set up Littleton, and he was so transported with joy for his victory, that he writ a short account of his success upon an open piece of paper and sent it as the news of Blenheim came to your Grace.

Besides this victory at Chichester the Whigs also ousted Tories at Maidstone, Queenborough, Rochester, Westminster and Woodstock, though the Tories held off Whig attacks at Banbury and Warwick.

The only one of these results to give the Tories any real encouragement was that for Suffolk. Nevertheless, for a Tacker to defeat a Whig knight of the shire was a tremendous fillip for High-Church morale, especially as Suffolk was the first of the contested counties to announce its results, and this seemed to augur well for other popular elections. The Tories therefore made the most of it. 'The poll ended on Wednesday night', wrote Dyer on 12 May,

> when 'twas found that Sir Rob Davers had 2883, the earl of Dysert 2877, Sir Dudley Cullum 2318, Sir Sam. Barnardiston 2286 voices, so that the election was carried by a great majority, if you consider the terrible opposition that was made by the Low-Churchmen, and their friends the Phanaticks of all sorts, supported by the D [uke] of G [rafto] n, and the lords Cor [nwa] llis and H [erve] y. But this victory is owing in a great measure to the diligence of the clergy, of which 80 went and polled in one body, and as great singly, being not advertis'd of the design. And to pin the basket Sir Tho. Hanmer brought in a body of 300 horse at the sight of which the D— withdrew from the window, and all was

given up. And though the great cry of the Whigs was, and is, 'No Tacker', yet that is known to be the only word that is given out to the party. The true meaning is, No Church of Englandman.

The report that the Whigs had cried out 'No Tackers' was printed in *The Rehearsal of Observator*, which also claimed that the other side had shouted, 'No forty-eight, no Presbyterian rebellion, save the Queen's white neck.' This account was inevitably challenged in the Whig *Observator*, which kept up a running battle with the *Rehearsal* throughout this election.[8]

A more significant pointer to public opinion than the Suffolk election, however, was that for the City of London, which began on 14 May. Four candidates appeared on each side: Sir John Fleet, Sir Richard Hoare, Sir John Parsons and Sir William Withers for the Tories, Sir William Ashurst, Sir Robert Clayton, Sir Gilbert Heathcote and Samuel Shepheard for the Whigs. At the previous General Election three Tories and one Whig had been returned. From the start it was clear that the Whigs were going to carry all four seats in 1705. Even Dyer gloomily admitted that 'the four Whig candidates were declared to have the majority upon view, and are like to carry it upon the poll'. The poll took four days, being concluded on the evening of 17 May. As the Whigs had hoped and the Tories feared, the four Whig candidates succeeded by a clear majority. Heathcote topped the poll with 3346 votes, while Clayton, who obtained fewer votes than any of the other three, was 724 ahead of his nearest rival.

London proved to be far more typical of popular constituencies than Suffolk. In the English counties the Whigs made eighteen gains and lost only one other seat when Lord Edward Russell was defeated in Bedfordshire. They also gave the Tories a good run for their money in Kent, Northamptonshire, Warwickshire, Wiltshire and Worcestershire. Most of the larger boroughs followed London's lead, with the Whigs picking up two seats in Derby, and one in Bedford, Weymouth, Gloucester and Canterbury. There were, however, a few Tory gains in some large towns which went against the national swing. Thus they obtained a seat in Lancaster, Monmouth, Nottingham and York. The Nottingham result particularly delighted Dyer, who reported it on 22 May:

Mr Sacheverell met with terrible opposition from the Whig party
at Nottingham, which were supported by the D [uke] of
N [ewcastle], the lords K [ings] ton and H [o] w, and however
he carried it by a considerable majority, and they got him into the
chair before eleven, at which the Whigs look'd so simply as tho'
'twas past twelve with them. The management of this victory was
due in a great measure to the neighbouring gentry, and in a more
particular manner to the Honourable Gentleman Sir Tho.
Willoughby, who has carried divers other elections which he has
been at with equal success, as Newark, Retford and Leicester.

The last elections to be reported were mostly held in Wales and
the South-West. These were Tory strongholds and so the advantage
built up by the Whigs in earlier contests was to some extent offset by
the results announced in the last week of May and the first week of
June. Nevertheless, as Lord Halifax had noted on 15 May in a letter
to the duchess of Marlborough, 'the elections in the West were so
very bad before, that we must get ground considerably there'. He was
right as far as Cornwall was concerned, for where thirty-seven of the
county's forty-four members had been Tories in 1702, in 1705 it
returned twenty Whigs.

The final result was very close, the Tories having a slight lead
over the Whigs with about 267 Members in the new Parliament
against 246 on the Whig side. On the eve of the General Election
the state of the parties had been Tories 329, Whigs 184, so this
represented a substantial change in the balance of power.

An approximate estimate of the effectiveness of Government
influence in securing this result can be achieved by calculating how
many Tackers were indeed kept out of Parliament. The Tackers
can be identified from the eight division lists which claim to distinguish them. Excluding the Tellers, William Bromley and John
Buller, the eight lists, when collated, give a total of 136 names, which
is only two too many. This is a sufficiently close approximation to
the actual number on the division to justify placing considerable
confidence in the identification of the Tackers.[9]

Nine of their number had been knights of the shire in the six
counties whose lord-lieutenants were changed, and only four of these
regained their seats in 1705, though this included two in Oxfordshire
and one out of two in Cornwall, where Marlborough and Godolphin

personally intervened. From this point of view changing the lord-lieutenant of Suffolk was worse than useless, for where before only one knight had been a Tacker, two were returned in this election. The former Governor of Sheerness failed to get back in as Member for Queenborough, although taking the governorship of Chester Castle out of a Tackers' hands did not prevent his return for Chester along with a Tacking colleague.

The Cambridge University election was even more disastrous for the Government. Godolphin went to extraordinary lengths to secure the return of his son, who was opposed by Arthur Annesley and Dixey Windsor, an army officer. He searched the hedges and ditches of England and Wales to find M.A.s willing to travel to Cambridge to vote for Francis, sending away to London, Cumberland and the Isle of Wight for graduates. He was accused of threatening to take away Windsor's commission, which, if true, was a really vicious use of Government influence. Queen Anne herself and the Lord Keeper were prevailed upon to send down their chaplains to vote for Francis. Finally Sir Isaac Newton was persuaded to desist from the poll so that Lord Rialton could have the remainder of his votes.[10] All these measures proved fruitless, the final result being Annesley 182, Windsor 170, Godolphin 162, and Newton 117, 'by which', wrote Dyer, 'we see the sense of both Universities was for the Occasional Bill, and that they approved of the Tacking of it by choosing the same members that joined in it'.[11] Godolphin was staggered at this failure of his efforts: 'The loss of Mr Godolphin's election at Cambridge', he wrote to the duchess of Marlborough, 'is no small mortification to me, and I now have the same occasion to complain myself of the behaviour of the clergy, as some of my friends had before. . . .'[12] Lord Halifax further informed her grace on 22 May: 'I think my Lord Treasurer is truly moved at the behaviour of the University, and certainly there never was such usage offered to the throne, by a body that owe their dependence on the Crown. . . .'

Elsewhere the campaign against the Tackers was more successful. Although Sir Robert Davers was re-elected for Bury St Edmunds as well as being chosen for Suffolk, Sir John Thorold and Lewis Dymoke were kept out in Lincolnshire, while five others who had been knights of the shire were obliged to creep back into Parliament via small boroughs. Ninety of their number in all came back to Westminster after the election, so that the Government helped to purge the House of one-third of the Tackers despite its major setbacks.

The success of the ministerial election campaign, however, depended not only on the number of Tackers who were excluded, but also on the attitude of those Tories who were returned. How many moderate Tories would dissociate themselves from the ninety re-elected Tackers and support the ministry? Many ministers, especially those associated with Robert Harley, continued to be optimistic on this score right up to the eve of the session. Their hopes were jolted only when William Bromley, the leader of the Tackers, opposed the Government nominee for the Speaker's chair and received the votes of 206 Tories. Only about two dozen moderate Tories supported the ministry on this crucial occasion. It was then clear to most ministers, though Harley continued for some time to deny it, that the breach in the Tory ranks between Tackers and Sneakers had been repaired.[13]

In fact the distinction had been an unreal one ever since the General Election. It was dropped outside ministerial circles long before the final results were announced. Most predictions of the outcome were made in terms, not of Tackers, Sneakers and moderate Tories against the rest, but of Tories on one side and Whigs on the other, though allowance was made for a small number of Government supporters who might affect the overall majority in the event of a close contest between the parties. By the middle of May enough results were in for Dyer to estimate that 'upon the whole a sort of equilibrium seems to be between the parties'. When all the results were known an observer calculated that 'by the nearest computation [that] can be made the Whigs and Tories are equal, so that the Placemen will turn the balance'.[14]

In deciding which way to tip the balance the duke of Marlborough reckoned without the support of a substantial number of moderate Tories, despite Harley's assurances to the contrary. Writing to Lord Treasurer Godolphin the duke observed:[15]

Upon my examining the list you sent me of the new Parl: I find so great a number of Tackers and their adherents that I should have been very uneasy in my own mind, if I had not on this occasion begged of the Queen as I have in my letter, that she should be pleased for Her own sake, and the good of her kingdom, to advise early with you, what encouragement might be proper to give the Whigs . . .

Between the Tack in November 1704, and the choice of a Speaker in October 1705, the possible sources of parliamentary support available to the Government were narrowed down to the alternatives of reliance on 'Tackers and their adherents' and dependence upon the Whigs, despite ministerial attempts to keep more options open. Although it was possible to argue, as Harley did, that one reason for this development was the Government's mishandling of its relations with the moderate Tories, there can be little doubt that another explanation lies in the heat of the General Election, which cauterised the wounds in the Tory party. The exploitation by party propagandists of all the highly charged emotional issues released by the Tack vitiated the attempts of rational politicians to preserve the divisions it had created for their own advantage, and seriously impeded the Government s freedom of manœuvre. So far from Government policy dictating the outcome of a General Election, the result of the 1705 election dictated Government policy.

# CHAPTER EIGHT

# Conclusion: Election Results
# 1701–15

*. . . by a moderate computation the Whigs will be 299 and our
friends upon occasion, the Tories, 214*

$$\frac{}{513}$$

SIR JOHN COPE TO SIR ANDREW HUME,
22 June 1708

CONTEMPORARY verdicts on the seven elections held between 1701
and 1715 were, by and large, in agreement. The 1701 election was
generally held to have resulted in a Whig victory. Bonet, the Prussian
envoy, reckoned that they had gained a majority of seventy over the
Tories.[1] In 1702 the Tories were regarded as the victors. Bishop
Burnet estimated that 'the tories in the House of Commons were at
least double the number of the Whigs'.[2] As we saw in the previous
chapter, contemporaries considered that the 1705 election had
resulted in stalemate, so that the placemen held the balance. The
Whigs were the acknowledged champions in 1708, though calculations of their exact numerical strength varied. Among the most
optimistic was the earl of Sunderland, who calculated that they had
increased their majority by seventy.[3] The 1710 election prompted
most speculation, various estimates being given of the extent of the
Tory victory. A fairly common analysis, however, was that the
Tories outnumbered the Whigs by at least two to one.[4] In 1713
the Tory lead was held to have increased. A Whig's assessment of
his party's fate put the number returned from England and Wales
as low as between 150 and 160.[5] Finally in 1715 all observers agreed
that the Tories had been routed. 'So many Whigs', observed James
Stanhope, 'have never been returned since the Revolution', while

Charles Cathcart informed Lord Loudun in February: 'The elections have gone better hitherto than it was to be imagined. The Whigs reckon upon having a majority of a hundred and twenty in the House, without including any in that number but such as they are entirely sure of.'[6]

Historians on the whole have accepted the general verdicts of contemporaries, though they have disagreed to some extent about the size of the party majorities after each election. Thus some say the result of the 1708 election was a Whig landslide, others that it produced only a narrow majority for the Whigs.[7] Most controversy until recently concerned the outcome of the 1710 election and whether it gave the Tories a majority of three to one or two to one.[8] Of late, Professor Robert Walcott has denied the validity of calculating election results in terms of party gains or losses at all. According to his analysis it is more meaningful to calculate the effects of elections in this period on the numerical followings of seven 'party groups'.[9]

An application of the methods developed by Sir Lewis Namier enables us to test the verdicts both of contemporaries and of historians. This involves collating all the information available about the political allegiances of every Member returned to Parliament between 1701 and 1715. Above all it includes an exhaustive analysis of division and other parliamentary lists from the period. Such an investigation invalidates the conclusion reached by Professor Walcott that 'the "Tory" side in any one division inevitably includes many who at other times voted "Whig" and vice-versa'.[10] On the contrary, it reveals more consistent loyalty to party than was suspected even by historians who subscribed to the traditional two-party interpretation. The number of men returned to the House of Commons in Anne's reign totalled 1220. A few of these – 156 – do not feature on any reliable party lists. There remain over a thousand whose voting habits can be ascertained from them. When they are carefully examined, and palpable inaccuracies are discounted, 495 are found to have only voted Tory, while 439 divided exclusively on the Whig side. This leaves only 130 who wavered in their party allegiance significantly enough to have their apostasies recorded on parliamentary lists. Moreover, no fewer than 59 of these 130 waverers were Tories whose only recorded lapse from Toryism was to vote against the treaty of commerce with France in 1713, the issues raised by which, as is well known, split the Tory party asunder. Consequently only 71 Members returned to Parliament between 1702 and 1714 cannot be firmly identified as Tories or as Whigs. Most of these were placemen, such as William Lowndes, the Secretary of the Treasury, who sided with any administration whatever its party complexion.[11]

Using all the available evidence about M.P.s makes it possible to measure the state of the parties immediately after each General Election from 1701 to 1715.[12] Absolute precision is, of course, impossible.

There are a few Members whose politics are so obscure that their party allegiance can only be guessed. Then there are those who were not firmly attached to either party, but who voted with the Government. These upset nice calculations about the actual state of the parties, though they cause the least trouble if they are counted as having been on the prevailing side after each election. Thus a man such as William Lowndes can be counted as voting with the Tories from 1702 to 1705, with the Whigs from 1705 to 1710, and with the Tories again from 1710 to 1714. All in all, however, the anomalies presented by the obscure and the obsequious do not detract from the validity of calculating election results in terms of party gains and losses, since the vast majority of Members can be identified with confidence as Tories or as Whigs.

Whig optimism at the results of the 1701 election seems remarkable in retrospect, since the Tories emerged with an overall majority of about sixty-five. The sanguine hopes of the Whigs were, of course, shattered immediately after the meeting of Parliament, when Robert Harley carried the division for the Speaker's chair against their candidate. They had probably miscalculated because prediction was very uncertain at a time when politics were passing over the watershed from the confusion which had marked much of William's reign to the polarisation of parties which characterised most of Queen Anne's. A letter written by James Craggs shortly before William's death reflects the confused situation in this transitional period: 'in three years we have had three parliaments, great struggling in point of party, and notwithstanding all the management of the Court, which leans entirely to the interest of the Whigs, yet the Church (or Country) party have at this time an actual majority in the House of Commons'.[13]

The confusion evaporated in the 'sunshine days' which followed Anne's accession, and from then until the end of the period there was no great difficulty for contemporaries, nor need there be for historians, in calculating the outcome of elections in terms of Tory and Whig gains or losses. The Tories commanded a majority after the 1702 election of about 133, a comfortable majority, though not as large as that which Bishop Burnet attributed to them. In 1705 the Tories had a slight lead over the Whigs of about 21, though this was offset by the number of Tory placemen who were prepared to support the ministry even when it sided with the Whigs. The famous Whig majority of 1708 was in fact around 69, nothing like as big as the Tory lead of 1702, but respectable enough, especially with the addition of nearly all the Scottish seats. The even more celebrated Tory majority of 1710 turns out to have been 151. This was not even two to one. Indeed it was not as big a lead as the Tories gained at the next election, when they numbered approximately 363, giving them a huge majority of 213 over the Whigs.

Such a lead made their collapse at the polls in 1715 all the more dramatic. Within eighteen months of achieving far and away the biggest parliamentary majority of the period the Tories found themselves outnumbered by about 120. This fatal reverse is even more remarkable because the Tories had shown again and again that they had a natural majority in the country. When they won the 1710 election Henry St John observed:[14]

> What a difference there is between the true strength of this nation, and the fictitious one of the Whigs. How much time, how many lucky incidents, how many strains of power, how much money must go to create a majority of the latter. On the other hand, take but off the opinion that the Crown is another way inclined, and the Church interest rises with redoubled force, and by its natural genuine strength.

After 1715, however, the Church party of Anne's reign was never to rise again. The tremendous change in the political complexion of the House of Commons, ranging in eighteen months from a Tory majority of 213 to a Whig lead of 120, cannot simply be attributed to the inclination of the Crown. These party majorities were not merely manipulated by the Court, but rocked to and fro on the fulcrum of a volatile electorate.

One of the most important tasks which faces the historian of the electoral struggle in the years 1701 to 1715, therefore, is to account for this volatility. And this is a question which does not lend itself to a quantitive solution. The floating vote can to some extent be measured. Why people voted now Tory and then Whig can not. It is not possible to take an opinion poll of the dead. Various explanations can be advanced, but these can only convince by their plausibility and probability, not by statistical demonstration. In the end the historian has got to use his imagination.

It has been a major aim of this book to demonstrate that, if one weighs the various influences on voters instead of merely counting them, then party propaganda weighs most. Parliament was divided into two major parties on the basis of conflicting constitutional principles and political issues, concerning mainly the monarchy, the Church and foreign policy. These parliamentary parties appealed to the electorate for support. The bulk of the electors, especially if like Anglican clergymen or dissenters they had strong religious convictions, were as firmly committed to the Tory or Whig side as were their Members of Parliament, if not more so. But a significant minority shifted sides as they were variously persuaded to look favourably on one party and unfavourably on the other. By and large these voters seem to have shared Tory attitudes to the Church and the Continent, only siding with the Whigs when the succession appeared to be in danger. Thus the Tack did not injure the Tories in 1705 as decisively as the trial of Dr Sacheverell affected the fortunes of the Whigs in the subsequent General Election. Whig attempts to involve England in continental war in 1701 proved nothing like as popular as the Tory abandonment of the Continent in 1713. Only the Pretender's abortive invasion in 1708, and fears for the security of the Hanoverian dynasty in 1715, gave the Whigs clear overall majorities in the House of Commons.

# Appendix A
## THE BUCKINGHAMSHIRE ELECTION
## COMPACT OF 1715

*Lord Cheyne's memorandum, 11 Feb 1715*

The 2d & 3d of Septr 1713 P.12 at Westminster Regina Anne John Lord Viscount Fermanagh and John Fleetwood Esq were chosen Knights of the shire for the County of Bucks against a mighty opposition of Sir Edmund Denton and Richard Hampden Esq supported by the earl of Wharton and all the Whig Lords and Gentlemen in the county.

The above said Parliament by reason of the Queen's death in August 1714 was by law to sit but six months after her death and then a new Parliament was to be called, which was done accordingly. On which consideration I wrote a letter and sent it by my own servant very early in August to my Lord Viscount Fermanagh desiring his Lordship to join again with Mr Fleetwood for the next County election, which his Lordship answered in a letter without date by my own servant refusing to stand himself and desiring some other Gentleman in the same Interest might be set up in his room.

I being not pleased with his Lordship's answer sent my servant again with another letter earnestly pressing his Lordship not to decline the service of his Country but join again with Fleetwood for the County Election and praying leave to wait on his Lordship at dinner at Claydon, his Lordship's own house, hoping there to prevail with him. In answer to which my Lord Fermanagh writes very kindly and accepts my company at dinner but steadily persist in not standing for the county, vide his letter dated the 30 of August 1714. I went to Claydon I think the first Thursday in Septr, where I was most kindly received both by my Lord and Lady Fermanagh. I used all the arguments I could to persuade his Lordship to a compliance, but could not prevail, though my Lady Fermanagh was of my mind. Therefore I at parting prayed my Lady to be an advocate for the public in persuading his Lordship to serve his Country, and I would not then take his Lordship's present resolution for a refusal. Not hearing soon again either from my Lord Fermanagh or my Lady I wrote to her Ladyship the beginning of Septr to know if she could prevail on my Lord to join with Mr Fleetwood, to which I had an answer totally refusing; vide her Ladyship's letter Septr 21 1714.

Since which time I happened to meet Mr Alexander Denton at St James's palace at Court, who came to me and ask me what I intended to do touching the next County Election for Bucks. I gave a sudden answer, vizt. do as we did the last Election. 'What then' says Mr Denton, 'your Lordship is not for peace?' 'Yes I am and always was.' 'Why then' says he, 'why should not we join a Whig and a Tory and try to settle peace and good neighbourhood amongst us?' I knowing at that time my Lord Fermanagh's refusing to join Mr Fleetwood and that none else would, made answer that I should be glad to hear of any proposition towards peace and good neighbourhood. A few days afterward came Sir Richard Temple (now Lord Cobham) and Mr Alexander Denton to my house in Lisle Street on a day I was not at home, and repeated their visit twice the next day without the good fortune of seeing one the other. Therefore I went and returned my Lord Cobham's visit, finding him at home and Mr Denton with him, where the Lord Cobham was pleased to tell me that the Lord Wharton and several Lords of that interest had had a meeting to consult of fit persons for Knights of the shire at the next Election, that Mr Denton had informed them of what passed between him and me at St James, on which they determined that himself and Mr Denton should propose that the Whig Interest should name one, and the Tory Interest name one, whereby to avoid polling, strife and all animosities, great expence of money etc.

I readily embraced the proposition but could not determine the matter till I had acquainted the Gentlemen of the County which I would do by going into the Country forthwith. Which I did and invited to dinner at Bois all the neighbouring Gentlemen, communicating to them this proposition, who readily agreed since Lord Fermanagh had refused joining with Mr Fleetwood, and desired Mr Fleetwood might be the Tory man to join the Whig named by the other Interest.

I thought it most reasonable to consult Lord Fermanagh in this affair, and for that purpose Mr Drake and Mr Tho Eyrs of Burnham were so kind as to go with Mr Fleetwood and myself to Claydon, his Lordship's house, where we were very kindly received. Mr Fleetwood pressed his Lordship to stand the Knight of the shire with the person named by the other interest. My Lord with many compliments refused, but after much talk Lord Fermanagh said that Fleetwood should be Knight of the shire and he burgess of Agmondisham if Mr Drake and Lord Cheyne approved of him, which we did accordingly.

Now the sessions drawing on, which was to be held at Aylesbury the eighth of Oct 1714 I thought that the most proper time and place to come to a resolution. However, I came back to London before the sessions and had a meeting with Lord Cobham and Mr Denton who named Mr Greenville to be joined with Mr Fleetwood. No objection was to be made by either side, but Mr Hampden, who had the best interest of any Whig was to our great surprise dropped. On the seventh of Octr I met Mr Denton (by agreement) at the sessions, where we both declared what proposition was on foot for the peace of the County, vizt. that Mr Fleetwood and Mr Greenville should be chosen Knights of the shire, and prayed their approbation. To which Mr Hampden was the only person objecting in his own behalf pleaded long that he had served the County as Knight of the shire, and had often been at vast expences in standing candidate and thought it hard to be refused by a number of his own party upon an accommodation in the County to save expence and to avoid animosities, declaring he had offered his service in several places which was kindly received, and found great encouragement to be one of the candidates, which he then declared himself to be.

This public declaration of Mr Hampden's gave us Tories great uneasiness, suspecting insincerity on the Whigs' part, and that Mr Hampden and Mr Greenville were to be our Knights of the shire at the day of election, and we Tories laid asleep by the former proposition and unprepared to make any opposition. I not well satisfied with this declaration of Mr Hampden's returned to London and expostulated with Lord Cobham and others of that interest touching Mr Hampden's proceeding, that the Gentlemen of the Country knowing full well the long and entire friendship between the two families of Wharton and Hampden and also their personal friendship did much doubt Lord Wharton's sincerity and the rest of the party in this matter. Lord Cobham pawned his honour and credit to me that Lord Wharton and all those (which were many of great interest) who had signed a paper signifying their approbation of Mr Greenville and Mr Fleetwood would be sincere in opposing Mr Hampden, who had broke with them and deserved none of their friendship, vide Lord Wharton's reasons sent to the freeholders.

On this assurance I persuaded my cousin Fleetwood to go on with Mr Greenville, since we had none of our own Interest would join him, that Mr Hampden could not possibly carry his point against our own party and the Whigs joined in part with us. From the middle of Octr to the middle of Decr Mr Hampden and Lord Wharton made war, the former by printing, the other by writing (vide the papers) when by the intercession of some particular friends of Mr Hampden's there was an agreement made that Mr Greenville by Mr Hampden's interest should be chosen a burgess for Wendover and Mr Hampden be joined Knight of the shire with Mr Fleetwood, which was effected accordingly. Mr Greenville was chosen a burgess of Wendover the latter end of Jan. Mr Hampden and Mr Fleetwood chosen Knights of the shire on the 2d of Febr 1714[15] ... I perceived there was such a discontent throughout the whole County for want of an opposition betwixt the two parties (Whigs and Tories) that there were very few Gentlemen appeared on the day of Election on either side.

Huntington Library Ellesmere MS 10706a.

# Appendix B

## OCCUPATIONS AND PARTY
## PREFERENCES OF VOTERS

1. *London*, 1710
N.B. The votes of a small minority who voted across the party lines have
not been recorded.

| | TORY | WHIG | | TORY | WHIG |
|---|---|---|---|---|---|
| Apothecaries | 30 | 45 | Glovers | 19 | 78 |
| Armourers | 33 | 36 | Goldsmiths | 130 | 88 |
| Bakers | 61 | 59 | Grocers | 93 | 75 |
| Barber surgeons | 120 | 67 | Haberdashers | 11 | 153 |
| Blacksmiths | 95 | 70 | Innholders | 71 | 31 |
| Bowyers | 18 | 8 | Ironmongers | 34 | 39 |
| Brewers | 25 | 45 | Joiners | 118 | 95 |
| Bricklayers | 36 | 28 | Leathersellers | 65 | 70 |
| Broderers | 54 | 59 | Masons | 31 | 9 |
| Butchers | 121 | 40 | Mercers | 61 | 88 |
| Carpenters | 46 | 25 | Merchant tailors | 132 | 182 |
| Clothworkers | 51 | 59 | Musicians | 8 | 2 |
| Coachmakers | 24 | 23 | Painterstainers | 71 | 33 |
| Cooks | 49 | 21 | Pewterers | 26 | 53 |
| Coopers | 59 | 76 | Plaisterers | 53 | 20 |
| Cordwainers | 38 | 58 | Plumbers | 30 | 14 |
| Curriers | 46 | 36 | Poulterers | 50 | 21 |
| Cutlers | 54 | 36 | Saddlers | 39 | 24 |
| Distillers | 70 | 50 | Salters | 57 | 68 |
| Drapers | 40 | 87 | Scriveners | 23 | 7 |
| Dyers | 60 | 77 | Skinners | 52 | 78 |
| Farriers | 32 | 17 | Stationers | 115 | 80 |
| Fishmongers | 70 | 89 | Tallowchandlers | 57 | 65 |
| Fletchers | 6 | 7 | Turners | 47 | 41 |
| Founders | 46 | 49 | Upholders | 48 | 46 |
| Fruiterers | 13 | 19 | Vintners | 127 | 29 |
| Girdlers | 25 | 34 | Waxchandlers | 23 | 31 |
| Glassmakers | 13 | 20 | Weavers | 84 | 93 |
| Glaziers | 36 | 25 | | | |

2. *Norwich, 1715*

| | TORY | WHIG | | TORY | WHIG |
|---|---|---|---|---|---|
| Aldermen | 7 | 4 | Glaziers | 14 | 6 |
| Apothecaries | 6 | 4 | Glovers | 10 | 2 |
| Bakers | 48 | 57 | Goldsmiths | 1 | 0 |
| Barbers | 46 | 36 | Grocers | 23 | 31 |
| Basketmakers | 0 | 5 | Gunsmiths | 2 | 0 |
| Blacksmiths | 29 | 19 | Haberdashers | 2 | 4 |
| Bodymakers | 5 | 0 | Hatters | 4 | 0 |
| Booksellers | 0 | 1 | Hosiers | 4 | 5 |
| Braziers | 4 | 1 | Hotpressers | 11 | 19 |
| Brewers | 14 | 11 | Innholders | 13 | 3 |
| Bricklayers | 0 | 2 | Instrument makers | 1 | 0 |
| Butchers | 34 | 39 | Ironmongers | 2 | 1 |
| Buttonmakers | 2 | 0 | Joiners | 4 | 13 |
| Carpenters | 35 | 37 | Justices | 5 | 4 |
| Carvers | 1 | 0 | Keelmen | 2 | 0 |
| Chandlers | 1 | 1 | Knackers | 3 | 1 |
| Chirurgeons | 2 | 1 | Lath drivers | 0 | 1 |
| Clerks | 29 | 15 | Lime burners | 1 | 0 |
| Clockmakers | 0 | 2 | Linen drapers | 1 | 2 |
| Clothiers | 0 | 1 | Locksmiths | 3 | 1 |
| Coachmen | 1 | 0 | Maltsters | 2 | 1 |
| Coal merchants | 1 | 1 | Mariners | 2 | 1 |
| Cobblers | 0 | 1 | Masons | 35 | 21 |
| Collar makers | 1 | 1 | Mathematicians | 0 | 1 |
| Combers | 27 | 35 | Mayor | 0 | 1 |
| Comb makers | 3 | 1 | Mealmen | 1 | 2 |
| Confectioners | 2 | 1 | Mercers | 9 | 0 |
| Coopers | 13 | 5 | Merchants | 5 | 3 |
| Cordwainers | 82 | 96 | Millers | 1 | 0 |
| Curriers | 3 | 1 | Milliners | 1 | 4 |
| Cutlers | 3 | 6 | Notaries | 1 | 0 |
| Darnick weavers | 1 | 7 | Oilmen | 0 | 1 |
| Doctors | 1 | 2 | Painters | 3 | 1 |
| Drapers | 3 | 2 | Pattern makers | 0 | 1 |
| Dyers | 10 | 11 | Pavers | 0 | 1 |
| Esquires | 4 | 4 | Perfumers | 0 | 1 |
| Feltmongers | 0 | 2 | Pewterers | 0 | 1 |
| Fishmongers | 3 | 1 | Picklemen | 1 | 0 |
| Freeholders | 145 | 308 | Pinmakers | 0 | 1 |
| Gardeners | 2 | 1 | Pipe makers | 1 | 0 |
| Gents | 30 | 12 | Plumbers | 5 | 6 |

| | TORY | WHIG | | TORY | WHIG |
|---|---|---|---|---|---|
| Poets | 0 | 1 | Tailors | 71 | 52 |
| Porters | 1 | 0 | Tanners | 2 | 1 |
| Potters | 0 | 1 | Thatchers | 1 | 2 |
| Poulterers | 1 | 0 | Tilers | 0 | 5 |
| Printers | 1 | 0 | Tinmen | 3 | 1 |
| Pump makers | 4 | 0 | Town Clerk | 1 | 0 |
| Rabbit men | 1 | 0 | Trunk makers | 1 | 1 |
| Recorder | 0 | 1 | Turners | 2 | 3 |
| Saddlers | 4 | 3 | Twisterers | 6 | 6 |
| Salesmen | 1 | 0 | Upholsterers | 4 | 3 |
| Sheermen | 4 | 7 | Watchmakers | 1 | 0 |
| Shipwrights | 0 | 2 | Watermen | 0 | 1 |
| Shopkeepers | 0 | 1 | Wheelwrights | 1 | 0 |
| Shuttlemakers | 1 | 0 | Wine coopers | 1 | 0 |
| Sieve makers | 1 | 0 | Woolcombers | 0 | 2 |
| Soap boilers | 1 | 1 | Worsted weavers | 445 | 733 |
| Sugar bakers | 1 | 0 | Writing masters | 1 | 0 |
| Sword bearers | 1 | 0 | Yeomen | 8 | 11 |

# Appendix C

## SAFE SEATS, 1701–15

*Tory Safe Seats*

1. Constituencies with one Tory safe seat (64)

Berkshire, Wallingford, Marlow, Cambridge, Cornwall, Cumberland, Honiton, Exeter, Okehampton, Totnes, Dorset, Bridport, Shaftesbury, County Durham, Durham, Malden, Cirencester, Leominster, Hertfordshire, Lancashire, Preston, Leicester, Yarmouth, Peterborough, Nottinghamshire, Oxfordshire, Banbury, Ludlow, Taunton, Hampshire, Yarmouth (I.O.W.), Lichfield, Tamworth, Suffolk, Orford, Reigate, Chichester, Midhurst, Steyning, Westmorland, Appleby, Downton, Old Sarum, Salisbury, Worcestershire, Droitwich, Worcester, Pontefract, Ripon, Hythe, Beaumaris, Brecon, Cardigan, Caernarvonshire, Caernarvon, Denbighshire, Denbigh, Flintshire, Flint, Glamorganshire, Merionethshire, Montgomeryshire, Montgomery, Haverfordwest.

2. Constituencies with two Tory safe seats (25)

Amersham, Chester, Callington, Fowey, Launceston, Saltash, Derbyshire, Devon, Barnstaple, Dartmouth, Herefordshire, Newton, Stamford, Northamptonshire, Oxford, Oxford University, Somerset, Minehead, Christchurch, Newcastle under Lyme, Aldeburgh, Warwickshire, Warwick, Ludgershall, Westbury.

*Whig Safe Seats*

1. Constituencies with one Whig safe seat (46)

Bedfordshire, Bedford, Wendover, Tregoney, Cumberland, Cockermouth, Plymouth, Bridport, Weymouth, Bristol, Tewkesbury, Huntingdonshire, Maidstone, Grantham, Monmouthshire, Castle Rising, Higham Ferrers, Northampton, Northumberland, Berwick, Bishops Castle, Milborne Port, Andover, Petersfield, Winchester, Stafford, Bury St Edmunds, Guildford, Southwark, Arundel, Shoreham, Chippenham, Cricklade, Downtown,

Worcester, Beverley, Knaresborough, Northallerton, Richmond, Scarborough, Thirsk, York, Dover, Rye, Sandwich, Carmarthen.

2. Constituencies with two Whig safe seats (14)

Wycombe, Beeralston, Lyme Regis, Poole, King's Lynn, Morpeth, Wenlock, Newport, Eye, Bletchingley, Lewes, Heytesbury, Hull, Malton.

# Appendix D

## ELECTION RESULTS, 1701–15

N.B. These figures represent the state of the parties in England and Wales immediately after each General Election. Before they can be converted into actual votes in the House of Commons a number of factors have to be taken into account. First, all 513 Members were never present together in the House at the same time. Second, after 1707 the 45 Members for Scotland have to be considered. These usually increased the prevailing majority, but in 1713 they counteracted Whig losses south of the border. Third, the outcome of petitions upon controverted elections considerably altered the state of the parties at Westminster.

|          | 1701 | 1702 | 1705 | 1708 | 1710 | 1713 | 1715 |
|----------|------|------|------|------|------|------|------|
| TORIES   | 289  | 323  | 267  | 222  | 332  | 363  | 197  |
| WHIGS    | 224  | 190  | 246  | 291  | 181  | 150  | 316  |
| MAJORITY | 65T  | 133T | 21T  | 69W  | 151T | 213T | 119W |

# Appendix E

## CONTESTED ELECTIONS, 1701–15

It is impossible to compile a comprehensive table of contests for this period because no single source covers all constituencies. Information about them, therefore, has to be gleaned from a vast range of documentary evidence, and to deal adequately with this would require the resources of some such institution as the History of Parliament Trust. Though the Trust's work on the period 1715–54 is nearing completion, while labourers are toiling in the field from 1660 to 1690, it has not yet begun to investigate the years between the Revolution and the Hanoverian Succession. Even when it collates and combs all the available evidence for that era, however, we could not be certain that documentary evidence has survived for all contests which occurred in it.

The following table has been compiled, therefore, in the knowledge that more contests undoubtedly occurred than it records, and possibly many more. At the same time it rests on enough evidence to serve as a guide to the incidence of contests in the period covered by it. Most of the materials cited in the Bibliography at the end of this book helped in its compilation, but special mention must here be made to the work done by others in this field, particularly by local historians whose special knowledge saves the more general student years of work, and above all to those indefatigable researchers Browne Willis, A. B. Beavan and W. D. Pink, whose manuscript notes were of invaluable assistance.

The abbreviations refer to the type of constituency and the incidence of contests in them. 'cy' = county, 'bur' = burgage borough, 'cor' = corporation borough, 'free' = freemen borough and 'in' = inhabitant borough. These terms are explained in the Introduction. ' × ' indicates that a contest took place. During this period many constituencies were canvassed with a view to a contest which never resulted in the voters being polled. For the sake of precision only those contests are recorded which are known to have ended in a poll, or which almost certainly did as far as this could be ascertained from the available evidence.

Estimates of the size of the electorate in each constituency are also given, though these too have to be obtained from a wide range of evidence, and are sometimes conjectural. Poll-books are the most informative sources, but surviving examples relate to only 76 constituencies out of a total of 269. It is possible to obtain the number of votes cast at contested elections for a great many more constituencies from newspapers, letters, diaries and even, occasionally, from reports upon controverted elections in the *Journals of the House of Commons*.

Such figures have to be treated with care, since most constituencies returned two Members, and voters in them had two votes. It is therefore not a simple matter of totting up the total cast in order to arrive at the number who polled. At most contested elections there were either three or four candidates. When four candidates stood, then half the total number of votes cast gives a rough indication of the size of the electorate. Take, for example, the result at Bedford in 1705:

| | |
|---|---:|
| William Farrer | 385 |
| Sir Philip Monoux | 340 |
| Samuel Rolt | 225 |
| William Spencer | 151 |
| TOTAL | 1101 |

Half this total gives an electorate in Bedford of approximately 550 voters. It so happens that this number can be checked against a poll-book for this election which lists 573 voters. Simple division, therefore, seems to be a reliable enough method where the votes cast for four candidates are known.

When three candidates appeared, however, the calculation is not quite so simple. It is almost always possible to ascertain two candidates standing in partnership against one fighting alone. In this situation some voters gave both their votes to the partners, others 'plumped' for the single candidate, while others split their votes between the individual and one of the partners. Consequently the closest approximation to the number of electors can be obtained if one takes first the votes cast for the partners, and subtracts the higher from the lower figure. One then deducts the result from the number who voted for the single candidate, and adds the remainder of his votes to the total cast for the partner with the higher score. This somewhat elaborate procedure can be illustrated from the result in Winchester in 1715, when the numbers on the poll were:

| | |
|---|---:|
| George Bridges | 67 |
| Lord William Powlet | 46 |
| John Popham | 34 |
| TOTAL | 147 |

Bridges and Powlet, both Whigs, stood against the Tory Popham. Deducting Powlet's votes from Bridges's gives 21; subtracting 21 from Popham's leaves 13; 13 plus 67 comes to 80. This deduction can also be checked against a

poll-book which shows that exactly 80 people voted in this election, 46 for
Powlet and Bridges, 21 for Bridges and Popham, and 13 for Popham alone.
Where two or more results are known, the figure given in the table records
the biggest number polled.

There remain some sixty constituencies for which no contemporary polls
are recorded either in full or in summary. The size of the electorates in
these, therefore, as to be inferred from other sources. Where an electorate
has been ascertained from inference, the estimated size is queried in the table.
Fortunately the historian is not left completely in the dark, for some of the
information he seeks is to be found in the papers of the indefatigable antiquarian Browne Willis, much of it published in his *Notitia Parliamentaria*.
The first two volumes of this work appeared in 1715 and 1716, and while
the third was not published until 1750 it was based on earlier information
about constituencies, now preserved among his manuscripts in the Bodleian
library. The gaps in Willis's work can be made good only by reference to
similar studies for later periods, such as T. H. B. Oldfield's *History of the
Boroughs of Great Britain* (1792) and the History of Parliament's first
volume on *The Commons 1754–1790* (1964). Invaluable compilations though
these are, it would be unfortunate if one had to fall back on them for more
than a handful of constituencies, since in many the size of the electorate
changed between the early and the later eighteenth century.

| Constituency | Type | Size | 1701 | 1702 | 1705 | 1708 | 1710 | 1713 | 1715 | By-elections |
|---|---|---|---|---|---|---|---|---|---|---|
| BEDFORDSHIRE | cy | 2500 | | | × | × | × | × | × | |
| Bedford | in | 700 | | | × | | × | × | × | |
| BERKSHIRE | cy | 3000 | | × | × | | × | | | |
| Abingdon | in | 500 | × | | × | × | | | | |
| Reading | in | 1000 | | | | × | | × | × | |
| Wallingford | in | 130 | × | | × | | × | × | × | 1709; 1714 |
| Windsor | in | 250 | | | | | | × | × | 1711 |
| BUCKS | cy | 5000 | × | × | × | | × | × | | 1704 |
| Amersham | in | 180 | × | | × | | | | | |
| Aylesbury | in | 300 | × | × | × | × | × | × | × | 1704; 1709 |
| Buckingham | cor | 13 | | × | | | × | × | × | 1705 |
| Marlow | in | 140 | | × | | × | × | × | × | |
| Wendover | in | 120 | | × | × | | × | | × | |
| Wycombe | free | 100 | | × | | | | | | |
| CAMBRIDGE Co. | cy | 3250 | | | × | | × | | × | |
| Cantab. Univ. | M.A.s | 320 | × | | × | | × | | | |
| Cambridge | free | 320 | | | × | × | | | × | 1709 |
| CHESHIRE | cy | 5500 | × | × | × | | × | | × | |
| Chester | free | ?1000 | × | | | | | | | |
| CORNWALL | cy | 2000 | | | × | | × | | | |
| Bodmin | cor | 37 | | | | × | | | | 1706 |
| Bossiney | free | ?20 | | | | | | | | |
| Callington | in | ?80 | | | | | | | | |
| Camelford | cor | 25 | | | | × | | | | 1711 |
| Fowey | in | ?50 | × | × | | × | | | | |

| Constituency | Type | Size | 1701 | 1702 | 1705 | 1708 | 1710 | 1713 | 1715 | By-elections |
|---|---|---|---|---|---|---|---|---|---|---|
| Grampound | free | ?50 | | | | | | | | |
| Helston | free | 50 | | | | | | | | 1714 |
| Launceston | free | 90 | | | | | | | × | |
| Liskeard | free | ?100 | | | | | | | | |
| E. Looe | free | ?70 | | | | | | | | |
| W. Looe | free | ?60 | | | | | | | | |
| Lostwithiel | cor | 24 | × | | × | × | × | | | |
| Mitchell | in | 40 | × | × | × | | | × | | |
| Newport | in | ?60 | | | | | | | | |
| Penryn | in | ?100 | | | | | × | | | 1714 |
| St Germans | in | ?50 | | | | | | | | |
| St Ives | in | 200 | × | × | × | × | × | × | | |
| St Mawes | free | ?30 | × | | | | | | | |
| Saltash | bur | 56 | | | | | | × | × | |
| Tregoney | in | 160 | × | | | | | | | 1710; 1713 |
| Truro | cor | 25 | | | | | | | | |
| CUMBERLAND | cy | 2000 | | × | | | | | | |
| Carlisle | free | 450 | × | × | × | | × | | | |
| Cockermouth | bur | 300 | × | × | × | | × | × | × | 1711 |
| DERBYSHIRE | cy | 3000 | × | | | | | | | |
| Derby | free | 650 | × | | × | | × | | × | 1710 |
| DEVON | cy | 3000 | | | | | | | | 1712 |
| Ashburton | bur | 160 | | | × | × | × | × | | 1708 |
| Barnstaple | free | ?200 | | | | | | | | |
| Beeralston | bur | ?70 | | | | | | | | |
| Dartmouth | free | 100 | | | | | | | × | |
| Exeter | free | 1200 | × | | | × | | | | 1708 |
| Honiton | in | 400 | | | × | | × | × | × | |
| Okehampton | free | 250 | | | × | | × | | | |
| Plymouth | free | ?320 | | | | | | | | |
| Plympton | free | 90 | | × | × | | | | | |
| Tavistock | bur | 110 | × | × | | | × | | × | 1703 |
| Tiverton | cor | 26 | | | | | × | | | 1710 |
| Totnes | free | 60 | | | | × | × | | | |
| DORSET | cy | ?3000 | | | | | | | | |
| Bridport | in | ?200 | | | | | | | × | |
| Corfe Castle | bur | ?250 | × | | | | | | × | |
| Dorchester | in | 280 | | | × | | × | × | | |
| Lyme Regis | free | ?100 | × | | | × | | | | |
| Poole | free | ?100 | | | | × | | | | |
| Shaftesbury | in | 270 | | | | | | × | × | |
| Wareham | in | ?150 | | | | | | | | |
| Weymouth | bur | 960 | | | × | × | × | × | | 1711 |
| Co. DURHAM | cy | 1000 | × | | | | | | | |
| Durham | free | 1100 | | | × | | × | | | 1712 |
| ESSEX | cy | 5250 | × | × | × | | × | | | |
| Colchester | free | 1260 | | × | × | × | × | × | × | 1705 |
| Harwich | cor | 32 | | | | × | | × | | 1708; 1714 |
| Maldon | free | 360 | × | | | | | | × | |
| GLOS. | cy | 5900 | × | × | × | × | × | × | × | |
| Bristol | free | 3900 | × | | × | | × | × | × | |

| Constituency | Type | Size | 1701 | 1702 | 1705 | 1708 | 1710 | 1713 | 1715 | By-elections |
|---|---|---|---|---|---|---|---|---|---|---|
| Cirencester | in | 600 | X | | X | X | X | X | | 1709 |
| Gloucester | free | 1400 | X | X | | | X | X | X | 1709 |
| Tewkesbury | free | ?500 | | | | | | | | 1714 |
| HEREFORDSHIRE | cy | 4000 | | | | X | X | | | |
| Hereford | free | 1200 | X | | | X | X | | X | 1712 |
| Leominster | in | 300 | X | | X | X | | X | X | |
| Weobley | bur | 100 | X | X | | | | | X | |
| HERTS | cy | 3800 | | | X | X | | | X | |
| Hertford | in | 650 | X | | X | X | X | X | X | |
| St Albans | free | 600 | X | X | X | X | | X | X | |
| HUNTS | cy | 2000 | | | | | X | X | | |
| Huntingdon | free | 130 | | X | X | | X | | | |
| KENT | cy | 6200 | X | | X | X | X | X | X | |
| Canterbury | free | 1000 | | | | X | X | X | X | |
| Maidstone | free | 900 | X | X | X | X | X | | X | |
| Queenborough | free | 60 | | | X | | X | X | X | |
| Rochester | free | 600 | X | | X | X | | | X | |
| LANCS | cy | 3000 | | | X | | | | | |
| Clitheroe | bur | 90 | | X | | | | X | X | 1706 |
| Lancaster | free | ?1000 | | X | | | | | | |
| Liverpool | free | 860 | X | | X | X | X | X | | |
| Newton | bur | ?100 | | | | | | | | |
| Preston | in | 900 | | X | | | X | X | X | 1706 |
| Wigan | free | 200 | X | X | | X | | X | X | |
| LEICS | cy | 4700 | | X | | X | | | X | 1707 |
| Leicester | in | 1200 | | | X | | | | | |
| LINCS | cy | 4500 | | | X | | X | | | |
| Boston | free | 180 | | | | | | X | | 1711; 1712 |
| Grantham | free | 320 | X | | | | X | | X | |
| Grimsby | free | 100 | X | X | X | | X | X | X | |
| Lincoln | free | 500 | X | | | | X | X | X | |
| Stamford | free | 2500 | | | | | | | | |
| MIDDLESEX | cy | 3200 | X | X | X | | X | | X | |
| London | free | 7500 | X | X | X | X | X | X | X | 1707 |
| Westminster | in | 5900 | X | X | X | X | X | | | |
| MONMOUTHSHIRE | cy | 900 | | | X | X | | X | | |
| Monmouth | free | 1980 | | | | | | | X | |
| NORFOLK | cy | 6000 | X | X | | | X | | X | |
| Castle Rising | bur | ?50 | | | | | | | X | |
| King's Lynn | in | 430 | | | | | | | | 1712 |
| Norwich | free | 3000 | X | X | X | X | X | X | X | 1703 |
| Thetford | cor | 32 | | X | | X | | | | |
| Yarmouth | free | 500 | X | X | | X | X | | | |
| NORTHANTS | cy | 6300 | X | X | X | | | | | |
| Brackley | cor | 33 | X | X | X | | X | X | | |
| Higham Ferrers | free | 90 | | X | | | | | | |
| Northampton | in | 1000 | | X | | X | X | | | 1704 |
| Peterborough | in | 350 | X | | | X | | | | |
| NORTHUMBERLAND | cy | 1200 | X | | X | X | | | | |
| Berwick | free | 250 | | | | | | X | | 1711 |
| Morpeth | free | 120 | | X | | | | X | X | |

| Constituency | Type | Size | 1701 | 1702 | 1705 | 1708 | 1710 | 1713 | 1715 | By-elections |
|---|---|---|---|---|---|---|---|---|---|---|
| Newcastle | free | 1400 | | | | | ✗ | | ✗ | |
| NOTTS | cy | 2300 | ✗ | ✗ | | | ✗ | | | |
| Newark | in | 490 | ✗ | | | | ✗ | ✗ | ✗ | 1712 |
| Nottingham | free | 1350 | ✗ | | ✗ | ✗ | ✗ | ✗ | ✗ | |
| Retford | free | 130 | ✗ | ✗ | ✗ | ✗ | ✗ | | | |
| OXON | cy | ?2600 | | | | | | | | 1710 |
| Banbury | cor | 26 | | | ✗ | | | | | |
| Oxon. Univ. | M.A.s | 330 | | | ✗ | | | | | 1703 |
| Oxford | free | 750 | ✗ | | ✗ | | | | | 1706 |
| Woodstock | free | 340 | | ✗ | ✗ | | | ✗ | | |
| RUTLAND | cy | 550 | | | | ✗ | ✗ | ✗ | ✗ | |
| SALOP | cy | 3600 | ✗ | ✗ | | | ✗ | ✗ | ✗ | |
| Bps Castle | free | 100 | ✗ | | ✗ | | ✗ | ✗ | ✗ | |
| Bridgnorth | free | 500 | ✗ | | | | ✗ | | | |
| Ludlow | free | 360 | ✗ | | ✗ | ✗ | ✗ | ✗ | | |
| Shrewsbury | free | 950 | | ✗ | | ✗ | ✗ | ✗ | | 1710 |
| Wenlock | free | ?100 | | | | | ✗ | | | |
| SOMERSET | cy | 4000 | | ✗ | ✗ | | | | ✗ | |
| Bath | cor | 33 | | ✗ | ✗ | ✗ | ✗ | | ✗ | 1707 |
| Bridgwater | in | ?300 | | | | | | | | |
| Ilchester | in | 130 | | ✗ | | ✗ | | | ✗ | |
| Milborne Port | in | 50 | ✗ | ✗ | ✗ | ✗ | ✗ | | | |
| Minehead | in | 340 | | | | | | ✗ | | |
| Taunton | in | 1000 | | ✗ | | | ✗ | | ✗ | |
| Wells | free | 60 | | | | | ✗ | | | |
| HANTS | cy | 4500 | | | ✗ | ✗ | ✗ | ✗ | | |
| Andover | cor | 24 | ✗ | ✗ | | | | ✗ | | |
| Christchurch | in | ?70 | | | | | ✗ | | | |
| Lymington | free | 40 | | | | | ✗ | | | |
| Newport | cor | 24 | | | | | | | ✗ | |
| Newtown | bur | ?40 | | | | | | | | |
| Petersfield | bur | ?150 | | | | | | | | |
| Portsmouth | free | 100 | | | | | ✗ | | | 1710 |
| Southampton | free | 300 | | | ✗ | | | | ✗ | 1708 |
| Stockbridge | in | ?60 | | | ✗ | | | ✗ | | |
| Whitchurch | bur | 80 | | ✗ | ✗ | ✗ | ✗ | | ✗ | 1708 |
| Winchester | free | 80 | | | | | | | ✗ | |
| Yarmouth | free | ?60 | | | | | | | | |
| STAFFS | cy | ?5000 | | | | ✗ | | | ✗ | |
| Lichfield | bur | 480 | | ✗ | | | ✗ | | ✗ | |
| Newcastle | free | 340 | | | ✗ | ✗ | | ✗ | ✗ | 1703 |
| Stafford | free | 270 | | | | | ✗ | | | |
| Tamworth | in | 280 | | | ✗ | ✗ | ✗ | ✗ | | |
| SUFFOLK | cy | 5200 | | ✗ | ✗ | | ✗ | | | 1707 |
| Aldeburgh | free | 80 | | | | ✗ | | ✗ | ✗ | |
| Bury | cor | 37 | ✗ | ✗ | | | | ✗ | | 1703 |
| Dunwich | free | 130 | | | | ✗ | ✗ | | ✗ | |
| Eye | in | ?200 | | | | | | | | |
| Ipswich | free | 480 | ✗ | ✗ | | ✗ | ✗ | ✗ | | 1707 |
| Orford | free | 90 | ✗ | ✗ | | ✗ | ✗ | | | |
| Sudbury | free | 800 | | ✗ | ✗ | ✗ | ✗ | | | 1703 |

| Constituency | Type | Size | 1701 | 1702 | 1705 | 1708 | 1710 | 1713 | 1715 | By-elections |
|---|---|---|---|---|---|---|---|---|---|---|
| SURREY | cy | 4000 | X | X | X | X | X | X | X | |
| Bletchingley | bur | 80 | | | | | X | X | | 1702 |
| Gatton | in | ?10 | | | | | | | | |
| Guildford | free | 200 | | | X | X | X | X | | 1714 |
| Haslemere | bur | 90 | | X | X | | X | X | X | |
| Reigate | bur | 240 | X | X | | | X | X | | |
| Southwark | in | 3500 | X | X | X | | X | X | | 1702;1712;1714 |
| SUSSEX | cy | 3200 | X | | X | X | X | X | X | |
| Arundel | in | 100 | | | | | | | | 1709 |
| Bramber | bur | 30 | X | | X | X | X | | X | 1703; 1704 |
| Chichester | in | 400 | | | X | X | X | X | X | |
| Grinstead | bur | 40 | | X | | X | | | | |
| Horsham | bur | 70 | X | X | X | X | | X | X | 1707 |
| Lewes | in | 200 | | | X | | X | | | |
| Midhurst | bur | ?100 | | | | X | X | | | |
| Shoreham | in | ?70 | X | X | X | X | X | | X | 1708 |
| Steyning | in | 80 | | X | X | X | X | | X | 1709; 1712 |
| WARWICKSHIRE | cy | 3200 | | | X | | | | | |
| Coventry | free | 1500 | X | X | X | X | X | X | | 1707 |
| Warwick | in | 350 | | X | X | | | | X | 1710 |
| WESTMORLAND | cy | 1150 | X | X | X | X | | | | |
| Appleby | bur | 100 | X | X | | X | X | X | | |
| WILTSHIRE | cy | 3200 | X | X | X | | | X | | |
| Bedwin | bur | 120 | X | | X | X | | | | 1707 |
| Calne | free | 60 | X | | X | X | X | X | X | |
| Chippenham | bur | 100 | | | | | X | X | X | 1705 |
| Cricklade | bur | 140 | | X | X | X | X | X | | 1714 |
| Devizes | free | 40 | | | | X | X | X | | 1706 |
| Downtown | bur | ?20 | | | | | | | | |
| Heytesbury | bur | ?50 | | | | | | | | |
| Hindon | in | 120 | | X | | X | X | X | X | |
| Ludgershall | bur | 100 | | | X | | X | X | X | |
| Malmesbury | cor | 13 | X | | X | X | | | | |
| Marlborough | free | 40 | | | X | | X | | X | 1705; 1708 |
| Old Sarum | bur | 10 | | | X | | | | X | |
| Salisbury | cor | 56 | | | X | | | X | X | |
| Westbury | bur | 50 | | X | | X | X | | X | |
| Wilton | free | 60 | | X | | X | X | | | |
| Wootton Bass. | in | ?150 | | | | X | | X | | |
| WORCS | cy | 2800 | X | X | X | | | | | |
| Bewdley | cor | 25 | | | X | X | X | X | X | |
| Droitwich | bur | ?40 | | | | X | | | | |
| Evesham | free | ?700 | | X | X | X | | | X | |
| Worcester | free | 1500 | X | | | X | X | X | X | |
| YORKSHIRE | cy | 9300 | | | X | X | X | | | 1706 |
| Aldborough | bur | ?70 | | | | | | X | | |
| Beverley | free | 400 | X | X | | | | | | |
| Boroughbridge | bur | ?60 | | | | | | X | X | |
| Hedon | free | ?70 | | | | | X | | | |
| Hull | free | ?700 | X | | | | | | | |

| Constituency | Type | Size | 1701 | 1702 | 1705 | 1708 | 1710 | 1713 | 1715 | By-election |
|---|---|---|---|---|---|---|---|---|---|---|
| Knaresborough | bur | ?50 | | | | | | | × | |
| Malton | bur | 260 | | | | × | × | | × | |
| Northallerton | bur | 200 | | | | | × | × | | 1705 |
| Pontefract | bur | 260 | | | | × | × | × | × | |
| Richmond | bur | 200 | | | × | | | × | × | |
| Ripon | bur | 160 | | | | × | | | × | |
| Scarborough | cor | 38 | × | × | × | | | | | |
| Thirsk | bur | ?50 | | | | | | | | |
| York | free | 1800 | × | | × | | | × | × | |
| CINQUE PORTS | | | | | | | | | | |
| Dover | free | 370 | × | | | | × | | | |
| Hastings | free | 80 | × | | | | × | | × | 1714 |
| Hythe | free | 50 | | | | × | × | × | × | |
| Romney | free | 30 | | | | | × | | | |
| Rye | in | 60 | | × | × | × | × | × | | |
| Sandwich | free | 450 | × | × | × | × | × | | × | 1713 |
| Seaford | in | 60 | | | | | × | | | |
| Winchelsea | free | 20 | × | × | × | | × | | | |
| ANGLESEY | cy | 700 | | | | × | | | | |
| Beaumaris | cor | 24 | | | | × | | | | |
| BRECONSHIRE | cy | 1200 | | × | × | | | | | |
| Brecon | free | 180 | | | | | × | | | |
| CAERNARVONSHIRE | cy | 500 | | | | | | × | × | |
| Caernarvon | free | ?700 | | | | | | × | | |
| CARDIGANSHIRE | cy | 750 | | | | × | × | | × | |
| Cardigan | free | ?1000 | × | | | | | | | **1710** |
| CARMARTHENSHIRE | cy | 1200 | × | | | | × | | × | |
| Carmarthen | free | ?500 | | | | | | | | |
| DENBIGHSHIRE | cy | ?2000 | | | | | | | | |
| Denbigh | free | 1400 | | | | | | | × | |
| FLINTSHIRE | cy | 820 | | × | | | | | | |
| Flint | free | ?1000 | | | | | | | | |
| GLAMORGANSHIRE | cy | 1500 | | | | × | | | | |
| Cardiff | free | ?1000 | | | | × | | | | |
| MERIONETHSHIRE | cy | ?600 | | | | | | | | |
| MONTGOMERYSHIRE | cy | ?1300 | | | | | | | | |
| Montgomery | free | 80 | | | × | | | | × | |
| PEMBROKESHIRE | cy | 1500 | | | | | × | | × | |
| Haverfordwest | in | 400 | | | | | | | × | |
| Pembroke | free | 600 | | | | | × | | × | |
| RADNORSHIRE | cy | 1000 | | | | | | | × | |
| Radnor | in | 600 | | | | | | | × | |

# Bibliography

## I. Primary Sources

### 1. POLL-BOOKS

BEDFORDSHIRE. 1705, 1715: County Record Office, Bedford (OR1823, 1825; HY964).

BEDFORD. 1705: County Record Office, Bedford (GY8/3).

WINDSOR. 1711: County Record Office, Reading (D/EN F23/2).

BUCKINGHAMSHIRE. 1701, 1702: Buckinghamshire Archaeological Society, Aylesbury. 1705: Guildhall Library, London. 1710, 1713: County Record Office, Aylesbury.

BUCKINGHAM. 1713: Bodleian Library, Oxford (*Parliamentary Papers of William Bromley*, IV 12).

CAMBRIDGESHIRE. 1705: Guildhall Library, London.

CAMBRIDGE UNIVERSITY. 1702, 1705, 1710, 1715: University Archives, Cambridge.

CHESHIRE. 1702, 1705: University College of North Wales, Bangor (Mostyn MSS 8423–7). 1715: County Record Office, Chester.

CORNWALL. 1710: County Record Office, Truro (Carew-Pole MS CO/CC/17).

MITCHELL 1705: County Record Office, Exeter (Fortescue 1262 M/ Elections 1). 1713: County Record Office, Truro (23M/SE2/2/b).

COCKERMOUTH. 1701, 1702, 1705, 1710, 1711, 1713, 1715: County Record Office, Carlisle (D/Lec. 107).

DERBYSHIRE. 1701: County Record Office, Matlock.

DERBY. 1701, 1710: Central Library, Wardwick, Derby.

PLYMPTON. 1702: *Report and Transactions of the Devon Association*, XIX (1887) 657–8.

TAVISTOCK. 1715: County Record Office, Exeter (Bedford Collection 1258M).

DORCHESTER. 1705: County Record Office, Dorchester (Fox–Strangways MSS).

ESSEX. 1702: Guildhall Library, London. 1710: County Record Office, Chelmsford.

GLOUCESTERSHIRE. 1710 (incomplete): *Transactions of the Bristol and Gloucestershire Archaeological Society* (1936) pp. 195–6. 1715: Guildhall Library, London.

BRISTOL. 1715: Guildhall Library, London.

HAMPSHIRE. 1705: University Library, Southampton. 1710, 1713: Bodleian Library, Oxford.

PORTSMOUTH. 1713, 1715: Guildhall Library, Portsmouth.

SOUTHAMPTON. 1705: Blenheim Palace (MSS F1–16).

WINCHESTER. 1715: Public Library, Winchester.

HEREFORDSHIRE. 1710: Hereford City Library (LC3500).

HERTFORDSHIRE. 1715: County Record Office, Hertford (QPE5).

HERTFORD. 1701, 1705, 1708, 1710, 1715: Hertford City Records, volume XXIII.

KENT. 1713, 1715: County Record Office, Maidstone (Q/RPe 1).

QUEENBOROUGH. 1715: County Record Office, Maidstone (Qb/RPr).

LANCASHIRE. 1705 (incomplete): John Rylands Library, Manchester (Crawford MSS).

CLITHEROE. 1713 (incomplete): County Record Office, Preston (MBC/83).

WIGAN. 1702, 1708: John Rylands Library, Manchester (Crawford MSS).

LEICESTERSHIRE. December 1707: University Library, Cambridge University (Add. MS 2520, folios 200–23).

GRANTHAM. 1715: County Record Office, Lincoln (Anc.13B2).

MIDDLESEX. 1705 (index), 1713: Guildhall Library, London.

LONDON. 1710: Guildhall Library, London.

MONMOUTHSHIRE. 1708: National Library of Wales, Aberystwyth (Bute MS 126/V/156).

MONMOUTH. 1715: Society of Genealogists, London.

NORFOLK. 1702, 1715: Guildhall Library, London.

NORWICH. 1710, 1715: Guildhall Library, London.

THETFORD. 1702: HMC *Various Collections*, VII 148.

NORTHAMPTONSHIRE. 1702, 1705: *Copies of the Polls taken at the Several Elections for Members to represent the County of Northampton in Parliament* (1832).

BRACKLEY. 1702, 1705, 1710 (incomplete), 1713: County Record Office, Northampton (Ellesmere (Brackley) Collection 171/3/3–5).

NORTHUMBERLAND. 1705 (incomplete): County Record Office, Gosforth (Delaval MSS). 1710: Society of Genealogists, London.

F

MORPETH. 1702: HMC 13th Report (App. part vi, *Delaval MSS*, p. 190).

NEWCASTLE UPON TYNE. 1715: West Riding Record Office, Leeds (BW/P10).

NOTTINGHAMSHIRE. 1710: *Thoroton Society Record Series*, XVIII (1958).

NOTTINGHAM. 1710: *Thoroton Society Record Series*, XVIII (1958). 1713: Nottingham Public Library (M688).

RUTLAND. 1710, 1713: Leics and Rutland Record Office, Leicester (Finch MSS, box 4969).

SALOP. 1702, 1710: National Library of Wales, Aberystwyth (Aston Hall MSS 4403, 4405). 1713, 1715: County Record Office, Shrewsbury.

LUDLOW. 1705, 1708, 1713: William Salt Library, Stafford (D1788/58/32).

WENLOCK. 1710: County Record Office, Shrewsbury (Forester Records).

SOMERSET. 1715: County Record Office, Taunton.

BATH. 1710: County Record Office, Gloucester (Dyrham Park MS D1799x9).

LICHFIELD. 1710, 1715: Birmingham Reference Library (379746–7).

SUFFOLK. 1701: West Suffolk Record Office, Bury St Edmunds (613/767). 1702: Cullum Library, Bury St Edmunds. 1705: Society of Genealogists, London. 1710: East Suffolk Record Office, Ipswich (HD41.326).

ALDEBURGH. 1713: British Museum (Add. MS 22248, folios 13–14).

SURREY. 1705: Guildhall Library, London.

BLETCHINGLEY. 1710, 1713: County Record Office, Kingston upon Thames (60/9/25 and 26).

HASLEMERE. 1715: Guildford Museum (Losely MS 763/64).

REIGATE. 1701, 1702, 1710, 1713: County Record Office, Kingston upon Thames; W. Bryant, 'The List and State of Reigate Burgages'.

SUSSEX. 1705: *Transactions of the Sussex Record Society*, IV (1905) 21–67. 1713: British Museum (Add. MS 39290).

EAST GRINSTEAD. 1702: County Record Office, Maidstone (U29.057).

HORSHAM. 1701, 1705, 1713, 1715: W. Albery, *A Parliamentary History of . . . Horsham* (1927) pp. 40–1, 44, 54, 57–9.

WESTMORLAND. 1701, 1702, 1708: MSS of Mrs O. R. Bagot, Levens Hall, Westmorland. 1705: County Record Office, Carlisle (Lonsdale MSS).

APPLEBY. 1701, 1702, 1708, 1710, 1713, 1715: County Record Office, Kendal (Hothfield MSS).

WILTSHIRE. 1705: Guildhall Library, London.

CRICKLADE. 1710: British Museum (Add. MS 51319, folios 197–8).

SALISBURY. 1713: County Record Office, Dorchester (Fox–Strangways MSS).

WORCESTERSHIRE. 1715: Guildhall Library, London.

YORKSHIRE. 1708: The Minster Library, York.

PONTEFRACT. 1708, 1710, 1713: Nottingham University Library (Galway MSS). 1715: West Riding Record Office, Leeds (BF9).

RIPON. 1708, 1715: West Riding Record Office, Leeds (Vyner MSS).

NEW ROMNEY. 1710, April 1713, 1713, 1715: Kent Archives Office (Aep 18, 19).

SEAFORD. 1710: British Museum (Add. MS 33064, folios 197–8).

ANGLESEY. 1708: University College of North Wales, Bangor (Baron Hill MS 5524).

BRECONSHIRE. 1702: National Library of Wales, Aberystwyth (Penpont MS 2395).

PEMBROKESHIRE. 1715: National Library of Wales, Aberystwyth (NLW MS 6099E).


2. MANUSCRIPT SOURCES
A. *MSS in the British Museum*
Additional 4163, 4291, 4743, 5853, 6116, 7059, 7063, 7070, 7074, 7078, 9092–120, 10039, 11051, 11571, 17677WW–HHH, 19185, 19253, 21507, 22202, 22217, 22222, 22248, 22851–2, 24612, 27440, 28041, 28051–70, 28886–929, 29568–99, 31139, 31143, 31144, 32686, 33060, 33064, 33084, 33225, 33273, 33512, 34515, 34518, 34521, 34223, 35359, 35584, 36772, 37663, 38157, 39290, 40621, 42176, 47025–8, 47087, 49360.
Egerton 929, 1705A, 2540, 2618, 3345.
Harleian Misc. autograph 4712.
Lansdowne 773, 885, 1013, 1216.
Portland Loan 29.
Stowe 222–6, 354, 748.


B. *MSS in the Bodleian Library*
Additional A269, C217.
Ballard 4, 6, 7, 9, 10, 12, 15, 17, 20, 21, 31, 34, 35, 36, 38, 39, 45.
Carte 109, 117, 125, 233, 244.
English Hist. d150, Misc. e4, Misc. e180.
Locke c38, c40.
MSS Film 297, 298.
North B2, C9.
Rawlinson A245, A286, D174, D1207, Letters 40, 92 and 108.


C. *MSS in Record Offices*
(*a*) Bedfordshire Record Office, Bedford.
    MS WG2653.

(*b*) Berkshire Record Office, Reading.
    Neville MSS.
    Trumbull MSS.
(*c*) Buckinghamshire Record Office, Aylesbury.
    Claydon House letters (microfilm).
(*d*) Cornwall Record Office, Truro.
    Buller MSS, deposited by Sir John Carew-Pole.
    Johnson MSS.
    Malone MSS.
(*e*) Cumberland and Westmorland Joint Archives Committee.
    (i) The Castle, Carlisle.
      Carleton MSS.
      Leconfield MSS.
      Lonsdale MSS.
    (ii) Record Office, Kendal.
      Appleby Corporation Records.
      Hothfield MSS.
(*f*) Devon Record Office, Exeter.
    Drake-King Correspondence.
(*g*) Essex Record Office, Chelmsford.
    Braybrooke MSS.
    Dacre–Barrett MSS.
    Maldon Borough Records, D/B3/1–3.
    Lieutenancy Papers, DDKW. 01 and 02.
    Quarter Sessions Records, QSB. 24, 3.
(*h*) Gloucestershire Record Office, Gloucester.
    Dyrham Park (Blathwayt) MSS.
    Ducie MSS.
    Newton MSS.
(*i*) Herefordshire Record Office, Hereford.
    Bridges MSS.
(*j*) Hertfordshire Record Office, Hertford.
    Panshanger MSS.
(*k*) Kent Record Office, Maidstone.
    Sandwich Corporation Records.
(*l*) Lancashire Record Office, Preston.
    Kenyon Correspondence.
    Parker Correspondence.
(*m*) Leicestershire and Rutland Record Office, Leicester.
    Finch MSS 4950, 4969.
(*n*) Lincolnshire Record Office, Lincoln.
    Massingberd Correspondence.
    Monson Papers.
    Worsley MSS.

(*o*) Middlesex Record Office, Westminster.
  Jersey MSS.
(*p*) Northamptonshire Record Office, Northampton.
  Cartwright (Aynhoe) MSS.
  Ellesmere (Brackley) Collection.
  Finch MSS.
  Isham Correspondence.
  Westmorland (Apethorpe) MSS.
(*q*) Northumberland Record Office, Gosforth.
  Blackett MSS.
(*r*) Public Record Office, London.
  Shaftesbury Papers.
(*s*) Staffordshire Record Office, Stafford.
  Leveson-Gower Papers.
(*t*) Surrey Record Office, Kingston.
  Clayton Papers.
(*u*) East Sussex Record Office, Lewes.
  Ashburnham Letterbooks.
(*v*) West Sussex Record Office, Chichester.
  Winterton Letters
(*w*) Worcestershire Record Office, Worcester
  Pakington MSS
(*x*) Yorkshire West Riding Record Office, Leeds.
  Newby Hall MSS.
  Temple Newsam Correspondence.
  Vyner MSS.


D. *MSS in Institutional and Public Libraries*
(*a*) National Library of Wales, Aberystwyth.
  Aston Hall MSS.
  Bettisfield MSS.
  Bute MSS.
  Chirk Castle MSS.
  Llanfair and Bynodol MSS 96, 98.
  NLW MSS 530E; 1548F; 12172.
  Ottley MSS.
  Penpont MSS.
  Penrice and Margam MSS.
  Tredegar MSS.
(*b*) University College of North Wales Library, Bangor.
  Baron Hill MSS.
(*c*) Churchill College Library, Cambridge.
  Drax MSS.

(*d*) University Library, Cambridge.
 Cholmondley (Houghton) Correspondence.
(*e*) Tullie House Library, Carlisle.
 Bishop Nicholson's diaries.
(*f*) City Library, Exeter.
 Exeter Corporation Records.
(*g*) Public Library, Huddersfield.
 Whitley Beaumont Collection.
(*h*) Henry E. Huntington Library, San Marino, California.
 Ellesmere MSS.
 Loudun MSS.
 Stowe MSS 57 and 58.
(*i*) Leicester Museum.
 Braye MSS.
(*j*) Chetham Library, Manchester.
 Mun. A460: admission book of Lancaster freemen.
(*k*) John Rylands Library, Manchester.
 Haigh MSS.
 Legh of Lyme Muniments.
(*l*) University Library, Newcastle upon Tyne.
 MSS misc. 10. Clavering Letterbook 1712–34.
(*m*) University Library, Nottingham.
 Galway MSS.
 Hollis MSS.
 Portland MSS.
(*n*) Christ Church College Library, Oxford.
 Wake MSS.
(*o*) William Salt Library, Stafford.
 Dartmouth MSS.
 Swynfen Letters.

E. *MSS in private ownership*
(*a*) Alnwick Castle, Northumberland.
 MSS of the duke of Northumberland.
(*b*) Blenheim Palace, Woodstock, Oxon.
 MSS of the duke of Marlborough.
(*c*) Corsham Court, Wiltshire.
 MSS of Lord Methuen.
(*d*) Levens Hall, Westmorland.
 MSS of Mrs O. R. Bagot.
(*e*) Longleat House, Wiltshire.
 MSS of the marquess of Bath.
(*f*) Walton Hall, Warwickshire.
 MSS of Sir Richard Hamilton.

(*g*) Weston Park, Shifnal, Salop.
  MSS of the earl of Bradford.


3. PRINTED SOURCES

A. Reports of the Royal Commission of Historical Manuscripts, listed as in
  *Government Publications: Publications of the Royal Commission on
  Historical Manuscripts: Sectional list no.* 17 (H.M.S.O., 1961).
  Series 6, seventh report: MSS of Sir H. Verney.
  Series 7, 1, I eighth report, part i, section i: Marlborough MSS.
  Series 7, 2, I eighth report, part i, section ii: Chester Corporation and
    Braybrooke MSS.
  Series 7, II eighth report, part ii: Manchester MSS.
  Series 8, ninth report, part ii: Morrison MSS.
  Series 13, tenth report, appendix iv: Westmorland, Bagot and Stewart MSS.
  Series 15, tenth report, appendix vi: Luttrell and Bromley Davenport MSS.
  Series 19, eleventh report, appendix iv: Townshend MSS.
  Series 20, eleventh report, appendix v: Dartmouth MSS i.
  Series 22, eleventh report, appendix vii: Le Strange and Saville MSS.
  Series 23, 2, twelfth report, appendix ii and iii: Cowper MSS ii and iii.
  Series 24, 2, twelfth report, appendix iv: Rutland MSS ii.
  Series 25, twelfth report, appendix vii: Le Fleming MSS.
  Series 26, twelfth report, appendix viii: Atholl MSS.
  Series 29, 2, thirteenth report, appendix ii: Portland MSS ii.
  Series 29, 4, fifteenth report, appendix iv: Portland MSS iv.
  Series 29, 5: Portland MSS v.
  Series 29, 7: Portland MSS vii.
  Series 29, 8: Portland MSS viii.
  Series 29, 9: Portland MSS ix.
  Series 29, 10: Portland MSS x.
  Series 30, 1, thirteenth report, appendix iii: Fortescue MSS i.
  Series 31, thirteenth report, appendix iv: Hastings Corporation MSS.
  Series 32, thirteenth report, appendix vi: Delaval MSS.
  Series 33, thirteenth report, appendix vii: Lonsdale MSS.
  Series 35, fourteenth report, appendix iv: Kenyon MSS.
  Series 36, new series: Ormonde MSS viii.
  Series 37, fourteenth report, appendix viii: Bury and Grimsby Corporations
    MSS.
  Series 42, fifteenth report, appendix vi: Carlisle MSS.
  Series 43, fifteenth report, appendix vii: Somerset and Ailesbury MSS.
  Series 44, fifteenth report, appendix viii: Drumlanrig MSS i.
  Series 45: Buccleuch MSS i.
  Series 49: Sackville MSS i.
  Series 51: Leyborne–Popham MSS.

Series 52: Frankland–Russell–Astley MSS.
Series 55, 1: Various collections, I Lostwithiel Corporation MSS.
Series 55, 4: Various collections, IV Orford Corporation MSS.
Series 55, 7: Various collections, VII Dunwich and Thetford Corporations MSS.
Series 55, 8: Various collections, VIII Clements MSS.
Series 58, 1, 2, 3: Bath MSS i, ii, iii.
Series 60, 1, 2: Mar and Kellie MSS i and ii.
Series 63, 2: Egmont MSS ii.
Series 66: Ancaster MSS.
Series 75, part ii: Downshire MSS.
Series 76: Bathurst MSS.
Series 79: Lindsey MSS.

B. *Collections of Private Correspondence and Papers*
*The Letters of Joseph Addison*, ed. W. Graham (Oxford, 1941).
*The Letters . . . of Queen Anne*, ed. Beatrice Curtis Brown (1935).
*The Epistolary Correspondence . . . of . . . Francis Atterbury*, 5 vols (1783–90).
*Correspondence of George Baillie of Jerviswood*, ed. Lord Minto (Edinburgh, 1842).
'The Letters and Papers of the Banks Family of Revesby Abbey, 1704–1760', ed. J. W. F. Hill, in *Lincoln Record Society Publications*, XLV (Hereford, 1952).
*William Bromley's Parliamentary Papers*, 4 vols (Bodleian Library Collection).
*State Papers and Letters addressed to William Carstares . . . during the reign of King William and Queen Anne*, ed. J. McCormick (Edinburgh, 1774).
'Some Clavering Correspondence', ed. E. Hughes, in *Archaeologia Aeliana*, XXXIV (1956).
Rev. A. L. Browne, 'Lord Halifax and Malmesbury Election, 1701', in *Wiltshire Archaeological and Natural History Magazine*, XLVII (1933).
*The Correspondence of Sir Thomas Hanmer, Bart.*, ed. Sir Henry Bunbury (1838).
*The Harcourt Papers* (Oxford, 1880) II.
*Miscellaneous State Papers . . . from the Collection of the Earl of Hardwicke*, ed. Philip Yorke (1778) II.
*The Letter Books of John Hervey, first Earl of Bristol* (Wells, 1894) I.
'Memoirs of Edward Hopkins, M.P. for Coventry', ed. M. D. Harris, in *English Historical Review*, XXXIV (1919).
*The Memoirs and Secret Negotiations of John Ker of Kersland*, part III (1726).
Sir Thomas Lawson-Tancred, Bart, *Records of a Yorkshire Manor* (1937).
*Original Papers containing the Secret History of Great Britain*, ed. James Macpherson (1775) II.

Lord Manchester, *Court and Society from Elizabeth to Anne* (1864) II.

*A Selection from the papers of the Earls of Marchmont,* ed. G. H. Rose (1831) III.

*Private Correspondence of Sarah, Duchess of Marlborough,* 2 vols (1838).

W. Coxe, *Memoirs of John, Duke of Marlborough,* 6 vols (1820).

T. Heywood, *The Norris Papers* (Chetham Society, 1846).

*Letters from Humphrey Prideaux . . . to John Ellis,* ed. E. M. Thompson (1875).

B. Bathurst, *Letters of Two Queens* (1924).

*Letters and Correspondence . . . of Henry St John, Viscount Bolingbroke,* ed. G. Parke, 2 vols (1798).

*Letters of the Sitwells and Sacheverells,* ed. Sir George Sitwell (1901) II.

*Original Letters of . . . Lord Shaftesbury,* ed. T. Forster (1830).

B. Rand, *The Life, Unpublished letters and Philosophical Regimen of Anthony, third Earl of Shaftesbury* (1900).

*Letters from the Right Honourable the late Earl of Shaftesbury,* ed. J. Toland (1721).

T. Sharp, *The Life of John Sharp . . . Archbishop of York,* 2 vols (1825).

*Private and Original Correspondence of Charles Talbot, Duke of Shrewsbury,* ed. W. Coxe (1821).

*The Correspondence of Jonathan Swift,* ed. J. Elrington Ball (1910–11) I and II.

*The Journal to Stella,* ed. Temple Scott (1897).

*Verney Letters of the Eighteenth Century,* ed. Lady Verney (1930) I and II.

*Letters Illustrative of the Reign of William III from 1696 to 1708,* ed. G. P. R. James (1841) III. (*Vernon Correspondence.*)

W. Coxe, *Memoirs of the Life and Administration of Sir Robert Walpole,* 2 vols (1798).

*The Wentworth Papers,* ed. J. J. Cartwright (1883).

'The Correspondence of some Wiltshire Politicians *c.* 1700', ed. Lord Lansdowne, in *Wiltshire Archaeological and Natural History Magazine,* XLVI (1932).

*The Letters and Works of Lady Mary Wortley Montagu,* ed. Lord Wharncliffe (1861) I.

C. *Contemporary Diaries, Newsletters and Newspapers*
*Blundell's Diary,* ed. Rev. T. E. Gibson (1895).

*Burney Newspapers, 1701–1715* (British Museum).

'The Note-Book of Sir Walter Calverley, bart', in *Surtees Society Publications,* LXXVII (1883).

*The Private Diary of William Lord Cowper,* ed. E. C. Hawtrey (Roxburgh Club: 1895).

*A Collection of Several Paragraphs out of Mr Dyers's Letters* (1705).

James Etheredge, 'Some Observations relating to Myself', in *Miscellanea Genealogica et Heraldica*, NS I (1874) 211–15.

*The Diary of John Evelyn*, ed. E. S. de Beer (1955) v.

*Remarks and Collections of Thomas Hearne*, ed. C. E. Doble, D. W. Rannie and H. E. Salter, 4 vols (Oxford, 1884–97).

*The Diary of John Hervey, first Earl of Bristol* (Wells, 1894).

Narcissus Luttrell, *A Brief Historical Relation of State Affairs* (1857) v and vi.

'The Diary of Samuel Newton 1662–1717', in *Cambridge Antiquarian Society Octavo Publications*, XXIII.

*Nichols Newspapers, 1701–1715* (Bodleian Library).

'Bishop Nicholson's Diary', in *Transactions of the Cumberland and Westmorland Antiquarian and Archaeological Society*, NS I–IV (1901–5) XXXV (1935), XL (1939), XLVI (1964).

*The Spectator*, ed. D. F. Bond, 5 vols (Oxford, 1965).

*London in 1710 from the Travels of Zacharaias Conrad von Uffenbach*, trans. W. H. Quarrell and Margaret Hare (1934).


D. *Biographies and Histories written by Contemporaries*

A. Boyer, *The History of the Reign of Queen Anne digested into Annals*, 11 vols (1703–13).

A. Boyer, *The Political State of Great Britain 1711–1714*, 4 vols (1718).

G. Burnet, *History of My Own Time* (Oxford, 1833) v and vi.

R. Coke, *A Detection of the Court and State of England* (1719) III.

'Lord Coningsbie's Account of the State of Political Parties in the reign of Queen Anne', in *Archaeologia*, XXXVIII (1860).

Lord Cowper, 'An Impartial History of Parties', in John, Lord Campbell, *Lives of the Lord Chancellors and Keepers of the Great Seal of England*, IV (1846) 421–9.

*An Account of the Conduct of the Dowager Duchess of Marlborough* (1742).

J. Oldmixon, *The Life . . . of Arthur Maynwaring* (1715).

[R. Steele], *Memoirs of the Life . . . of Thomas, late Marquess of Wharton* (1715).


E. *Political Literature*

*A Collection of Addresses which have been presented to the Queen since the Impeachment of the Rev. Dr Henry Sacheverell* (1711).

*A Letter from a Freeholder in Leicestershire to a Friend in London* (1715).

*A Letter to the Gentlemen and Freeholders of the County of Dorset concerning the next Election of Members of Parliament for the said County* (1713).

*A Scheme of the Proportions the Several Counties in England paid to the Land Tax in 1693 and to the Subsidies in 1697 compared with the Number of Members they send to Parliament* (1698).

*A Vindication of the last Parliament in four Dialogues between Sir Simon and Sir Peter* (1711).

*Instructions to Freeholders drawn from Her Majesty's Most Gracious Speech from the Throne* (1713).

*Occasional Thoughts concerning our Present Divisions and their Remedies* (1704).

*The Electors' Right Asserted* (1701).

W. Bissett, *The Modern Fanatic* (1711).

*The Prose Works of Jonathan Swift*, ed. Herbert Davis, 13 vols (1939–64) vols III, VI, VIII.

[J. Oldmixon], *The History of Addresses* (1711).

*Poems on Affairs of State*, 4 vols (1716).

*A Collection of Scarce and Valuable Tracts*, ed. Sir Walter Scott, 13 vols (1809–15). [*Somers' Tracts.*]

*Political Ballads*, ed. W. Walker Wilkins, 2 vols (1860) vol II.


## II. SECONDARY AUTHORITIES

### I. GENERAL STUDIES OF CONSTITUENCIES AND ELECTIONS

A. B. Beavan and W. D. Pink, MSS notes on M.P.s and contests, John Rylands Library, Manchester, English MSS 296–306, 329–31.

T. Carew, *An Historical Account of the Rights of Elections* (1755).

E. Cunnington, 'The General Election of 1705' (unpublished M.A. thesis, London, 1938).

J. Greco, *A History of Parliamentary Elections and Electioneering* (1886).

Geoffrey Holmes, 'The Influence of the Peerage in English Parliamentary Elections, 1702–1713' (unpublished B.Litt. thesis, Oxford, 1951).

C. E. Langford, 'The British General Election of 1713', in *Essays in Modern European History by Students of the late Professor W. T. Morgan* (1946).

W. T. Morgan, 'An Eighteenth Century Election in England', in *Political Science Quarterly* (1922).

W. T. Morgan, 'Some Sidelights upon the General Election of 1715', in *Essays in Modern English History in Honor of W. C. Abbott* (1941).

T. H. B. Oldfield, *An Entire and Complete History, Political and Personal, of the Boroughs of Great Britain*, 6 vols (1792).

E. and A. Porritt, *The Unreformed House of Commons* (1909).

M. Ransome, 'Church and Dissent in the Election of 1710', in *English Historical Review*, LVI (1941).

M. Ransome, 'The General Election of 1710' (unpublished M.A. thesis, London, 1938).

M. Ransome, 'The Press in the 1710 Election', in *Cambridge Historical Journal*, VI (1938).

D. M. Reed, 'The Tackers in the Election of 1705', in *Essays in Modern European History by Students of the late Professor W. T. Morgan* (1946).

H. Stooks Smith, *The Register of Parliamentary Elections* (1842).

E. C. Whitworth, 'The Parliamentary Franchise in the English Boroughs during the Stuart period' (unpublished M.A. thesis, London, 1926).

Browne Willis, *Notitia Parliamentaria*, 3 vols (1715–50).

2. PARTICULAR STUDIES

*Parliament through Seven Centuries: Reading and its M.P.s* (1962).

D. Cook, 'The Representative History of the County, Town and University of Cambridge, 1689–1832' (unpublished Ph.D. thesis, London, 1935).

W. P. Courtenay, *The Parliamentary Representation of Cornwall to 1832* (1889).

R. S. Ferguson, *Cumberland and Westmorland M.P.s* (1871).

W. V. Ward, 'Members of Parliament and Elections in Derbyshire, Leicestershire and Staffordshire, 1660–1714' (unpublished M.A. thesis, Manchester, 1959).

*Reports and Transactions of the Devonshire Association* (1887–1941), vols XIX, XXVIII, XXXII, XLI, XLIII, XLIV, LXII, LXVII, LXVIII; articles on Devon, Ashburton, Barnstaple, Beeralston, Dartmouth, Exeter, Honiton, Plympton, Tavistock, Tiverton and Totnes by J. J. Alexander, the Rev. E. S. Chalk, Daphne Drake, the Rev. J. B. Pearson, J. Brooking Rowe, Major W. H. Wilkin and E. Windeatt.

W. R. J. Williams, *The Parliamentary History of Gloucester* (Hereford, 1898).

W. R. J. Williams, *The Parliamentary History of the County of Hereford* (Brecknock, 1896).

*Victoria County History of Huntingdon*, ed. W. Page and G. Proby (1932) vol. II, *Parliamentary History*.

Rev. J. Cave-Browne, 'Knights of the Shire for Kent, 1275–1831', in *Archaeologia Cantiana*, XX (1895).

W. D. Pink and A. B. Beavan, *The Parliamentary Representation of Lancashire* (1889).

J. M. Wahlstrand, 'The Elections to Parliament in the County of Lancashire, 1688–1714' (unpublished M.A. thesis, Manchester, 1956).

M. Coxe, 'Sir Roger Bradshaigh, 3rd Baronet, and the Electoral Management of Wigan, 1695–1747', in *Bulletin of the John Rylands Library*, XXXVII (1954).

*Victoria County History of Leicester*, vol. II, *Political History*, ed. J. H. Plumb (1954); vol. IV, *Parliamentary History*, ed. R. W. Greaves (1958).

H. H. Bradfer Lawrence, *Castle Rising and the Walpoles; a supplement to Blomefield's Norfolk* (1924).

E. G. Forrester, *Northamptonshire County Elections and Electioneering 1695–1832* (Oxford, 1941).

C. H. Hunter Blair, 'Members of Parliament for Northumberland,

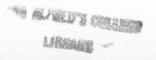

Newcastle, Berwick and Morpeth', in *Archaeologia Aeliana*, 4th ser., vols XXIII and XXIV (1945–6).

*Records of the Borough of Nottingham*, VI (Nottingham, 1914).

W. R. J. Williams, *The Parliamentary History of the County of Oxford* (Brecknock, 1899).

*Transactions of the Shropshire Archaeological and Natural History Society* (1895–1930) vols 2nd ser. VII, X, 3rd ser. II, 4th ser. V and XII. Articles on the representation of Salop, Bishops Castle, Bridgnorth, Ludlow, Shrewsbury and Wenlock by H. T. Weyman.

S. W. Bates Harbin, 'Members of Parliament for the County of Somerset', in *Somersetshire Archaeological and Natural History Society Publications* (Taunton, 1939).

H. C. Maxwell-Lyte, 'Dunster and its Lords', in *Archaeological Journal*, XXXVII (1880).

J. Toulmin, *The History of the Town of Taunton* (1791).

C. St Barbe, *Records of the Corporation of the Borough of New Lymington* (1848).

R. East, *Extracts from Records . . . of the Borough of Portsmouth* (Portsmouth, 1891).

J. C. Wedgwood, *Staffordshire Parliamentary History* (William Salt Archaeological Society, 1922) vol. II.

W. Albery, *Parliamentary History . . . of Horsham, 1295–1885* (1927).

W. Hooper, *Reigate, its Story through the Ages* (Guildford, 1945).

W. H. Hills, *The Parliamentary History . . . of Lewes, 1295–1885* (Lewes, 1905).

T. W. Whitley, *The Parliamentary Representation of . . . Coventry* (Coventry, 1894).

W. R. J. Williams, *The Parliamentary History of the County of Worcester* (Hereford, 1897).

P. Styles, 'The Corporation of Bewdley under the later Stuarts', in *University of Birmingham Historical Journal*, I (1947–8).

W. O. Bean, *The Parliamentary Representation of the Six Northern Counties* (Hull, 1890).

A. Goodere, 'The Parliamentary Representation of the County of York', in *Yorkshire Archaeological Society Record Series*, XCVI (1938).

W. R. J. Williams, *The Parliamentary History of the Principality of Wales* (Brecknock, 1895).

P. D. G. Thomas, 'Anglesey Politics, 1689–1727', in *Transactions of the Anglesey Antiquarian Society* (1962).

P. D. G. Thomas, 'Parliamentary Elections in Brecknockshire 1689–1832', in *Brycheiniog*, VI (1960).

P. D. G. Thomas, 'The Parliamentary Representation of Caernarvonshire in the Eighteenth Century: part i: 1708–1749', in *Transactions of the Caernarvonshire Historical Society*, XIX (1958).

# Notes

*Abbreviations used in the notes:*
Add.   Additional.
BM    British Museum.
HMC   Reports of the Royal Historical Manuscripts Commission.
NLW   National Library of Wales.
PRO   Public Record Office.
RO    Record Office.

## CHAPTER ONE: INTRODUCTION

1. The views suggested by Robert Walcott in 'English Party Politics 1688–1714', in *Essays in Modern English History in Honor of W. C. Abbott* (1941) and elaborated in *English Politics in the Early Eighteenth Century* (1956), though they held the field in general histories for a decade, were never wholeheartedly accepted by authorities on the period. They must be substantially rejected following the criticisms of them advanced by Geoffrey Holmes in *British Politics in the Age of Anne* (1967) and J. H. Plumb, *The Growth of Political Stability in England, 1675–1725* (1967).

2. E. Sussex RO, Ashburnham MS 843, pp. 383–4: Lord Ashburnham to John Pulteney, 21 Nov 1701.

3. Ibid. p. 388: Ashburnham to Whitlock Bulstrode, 5 Dec 1701.

4. Carlisle RO, Lonsdale MSS: James Lowther to William Gilpin, 3 Feb 1708.

5. *The Memoirs and Secret Negotiations of John Ker of Kersland*, Part III (1726) p. 205 (memo by Robert Molesworth).

6. 'English Advice to the Freeholders of England' (1714), in *Somers' Tracts*, ed. Sir Walter Scott, XIII (1815) 523.

7. *A Letter from a Freeholder in Leicestershire to a Friend in London* (1715) pp. 3–4.

8. See W. A. Speck, 'Conflict in Society', in *Britain after the Glorious Revolution*, ed. Geoffrey Holmes (1969) pp. 135–54.

9. E. G. Forrester, *Northamptonshire County Elections and Electioneering, 1695–1832* (Oxford, 1941) p. 24.

10. Berks RO, Trumbull MSS: St John to Sir William Trumbull, 2 June 1710; Chatsworth MS (Devonshire) 182.0: Thomas Pelham-Holles to the duke of Devonshire, 29 June 1713. I owe this reference to Dr H. Horwitz.

11. Blenheim MSS D1–32: George Lucy to Sunderland, 21 Feb 1705.

12. BM Add. MS 40794, folios 2–3.

13. Viscount Downe 4737, Sir William Strickland 3452, Conyers Darcy 3257, Sir Arthur Kay 3136, Thomas Wentworth 958.

14. *Letters of the Sitwells and Sacheverells*, ed. Sir George Sitwell (1901) II 86: William Sacheverell to George Sitwell, 30 Aug 1710.

15. BM Loan 29/302: Sir William Pole to Lord Oxford, 17 July 1712.

16. Northants RO, Isham Corr. 2431: Sir Justinian Isham to his son, 17 Feb 1711; *Verney Letters of the Eighteenth Century*, ed. Lady Verney (1930) I 323: Sir Thomas Cave to Lord Fermanagh, 11 Feb 1711.

17. Hertford City Records, vol. XXIII, folios 263–9.

18. BM Add. MS 27440, folio 140: Charles Allestree's memorandum book.

19. Bodleian, Ballard MS 10, folio 113: Simon Harcourt to Dr Charlett, 3 Mar 1701.

20. HMC *Portland*, IV 222: [Defoe] to Harley, 14 Aug 1705.


CHAPTER TWO: THE ELECTORATE

1. See Appendix E, pp. 124–6.

2. Most of the calculations in this chapter are based on the poll-books listed in the bibliography, pp. 132–5.

3. J. H. Plumb, *The Growth of Political Stability in England, 1675–1725* (1967) pp. 27–9, 34–47.

4. R. L. Bushman, 'English Franchise Reform in the Seventeenth Century', in *Journal of British Studies*, III (1963) 36–56.

5. E. C. Whitworth, 'The Parliamentary Franchise in the English Boroughs during the Stuart period' (unpublished M.A. thesis, London, 1926) p. 6.

6. Reading, Wallingford, Amersham, Wendover, St Ives, Honiton, Hertford, Leicester, Milborne Port, Taunton and Southwark. For the proceedings in the Commons relating to these boroughs, see T. Carew, *An Historical Account of the Rights of Elections* (1755) I 6, 278, 290–1, 323–4, 393–4; II 66, 101, 146, 193–4, 206, 218.

7. See below, pp. 54–5.

8. *Commons Journals*, XIII 416, 461.

9. Narcissus Luttrell, *A Brief Historical Relation of State Affairs* (1857) V 45.

10. Carew, op. cit. I 287–8.

11. 7 and 8 Wm III, c. 25.

12. Nottingham University Library, Galway MS 12259.

13. Browne Willis, *Notitia Parliamentaria* (1716) II 436.

14. Chetham Library, Manchester, Mun. A460. Admissions of freemen at Lancaster.

15. Carew, op. cit. I 177. The wholesale manufacture of freemen provoked recurrent complaints in petitions from unsuccessful candidates at Colchester.

16. HMC *Various Collections*, VII *Dunwich Corporation Records*, pp. 106–7.

17. *William Bromley's Parliamentary Papers* (Bodleian) IV 140.

18. *A Collection of Several Paragraphs out of Mr Dyers's Letters* (1705) p. 3.

19. 10 Anne c. 23.

20. Plumb, op. cit. p. 29.

21. This is the calculation given in P. Deane and W. A. Cole, *British Economic Growth 1688–1959* (1962) p. 103. It is higher than the figure of 5,500,000 arrived at by Gregory King in 1695, but though his estimate is usually accepted by historians it was probably low.

22. *A Scheme of the Proportions the Several Counties in England paid to the Land Tax in 1693 and to the Subsidies in 1697 compared with the Number of Members they send to Parliament* (1698).

23. See Appendix E, pp. 124–31.

24. Sir Lewis Namier, *The Structure of Politics at the Accession of George III*, 2nd ed. (1957) p. 159.

25. These figures ignore by-elections.

26. HMC *Various Collections*, IV *Orford Corporation Records*, p. 271; VII *Dunwich Corporation Records*, pp. 106–7.

27. There were about 145,000 forty-shilling freeholders in English counties. In Gregory King's table of 1695 – printed in Dorothy George, *England in Transition* (1953) pp. 150–1 – there are only about 66,000 eligible landowners down to 'freeholders, better sort'. Therefore some 80,000 of his 140,000 'freeholders, lesser sort' must have been entitled to vote.

28. Surrey RO, Somers MS B/50: W. Walsh to Somers, 26 Oct 1701. For London and Norwich see Appendix B, pp. 118–20.

29. W. Albery noted this trend in Horsham; *A Parliamentary History of Horsham* (1927) pp. 39–70.

30. Nottingham University Library, Portland (Hollis) MS PW2.291a: Whichcote to Newcastle, 17 Oct 1710; BM Add. MS 47026, p. 65: Sir Philip Parker to Sir John Perceval, 13 Oct 1710.

31. That in polling for Isham and Cartwright the Northamptonshire freeholders were voting Tory, while in polling for their opponents they were voting Whig is not just my assumption. See Blenheim MSS D2–9, where a contemporary, probably the earl of Sunderland, calculated their votes in precisely these terms.

32. *Review*, 29 May 1705. For an ambitious scheme to get the Kentish clergy to vote even more unanimously Tory see Ballard MS 49, folio 148.

33. BM Loan 29/321: Dyer's newsletter, 19, 21, 24 Oct, 4 Nov 1710.

34. Ibid. 28 Oct 1710. Dyer exaggerated the solidarity of the dissenting vote in this election, as Harley was able to use his interest with some nonconformists to persuade them to vote for the Tories in certain constituencies. See Mary Ransome, 'Church and Dissent in the Election of 1710', in *English Historical Review*, LVI (1941) 85–6.

35. Sir Thomas Lawson-Tancred, *Records of a Yorkshire Manor* (1937) pp. 265–6.

36. E. Sussex RO, Ashburnham MS 843, p. 380: Ashburnham to J. Friendly, 26 Nov 1701.

37. University College of North Wales Library, Bangor: Baron Hill MS 6749.

38. See G. C. A. Clay, 'Two Families and their Estates' (unpublished Ph.D. thesis, Cambridge, 1966) p. 63.

39. Leics RO, Finch MSS, box 4969: draft 2 Jan 1710.

40. M. Beloff, *Public Order and Popular Disturbances 1660–1714* (Oxford, 1938) pp. 50 and 55.

41. *Commons Journals*, XV 276–8.

42. J. Greco, *A History of Parliamentary Elections and Electioneering* (1886) p. 80.

43. W. Bissett, *The Modern Fanatic* (1710) I 8.

44. *London in 1710 from the Travels of Zacharias Conrad von Uffenbach*, trans. W. H. Quarrell and Margaret Hare (1934) pp. 146–8.

45. HMC *Portland*, V 346: Sir Robert Price to Oxford, 3 Sep 1713.

46. G. L. Cherry, 'The Influence of Irregularities in Contested Elections upon Election Policy during the Reign of William III', in *Journal of Modern History*, XXVII (1955) 109.

47. Geoffrey Holmes, 'The Influence of the Peerage in English Parliamentary Elections, 1702–1713' (unpublished B.Litt. thesis, Oxford, 1951) p. 137.

48. Anon., *Occasional Thoughts concerning our Present Divisions and their Remedies* (1704) p. 11.

49. Levens MSS: Carleton to Grahme, 11 Apr 1702.

50. Ibid. same to same, n.d. [1708].

51. How powerful is discussed below, pp. *79–85*.

52. Lord Campbell, *Lives of the Lord Chancellors and Keepers of the Great Seal of England* (1846) IV 427.

53. Cornwall RO, Malone MSS: circular letter, 15 Oct 1714.

54. Carlisle RO, Leconfield MS 110; printed in *The Divided Society*, ed. Geoffrey Holmes and W. A. Speck (1967) p. 123.

55. Gloucs RO, Ducie MS D340 c. 22.2: to Matthew Ducie Morton.

56. Sixteen were printed in *The Electors' Right Asserted* (1701); viz. Abingdon, Windsor, Buckinghamshire, Launceston, Lostwithiel, Shaftesbury, County Durham, Gloucestershire, Bristol, London, Westminster, Southwark, Sussex, Wiltshire, Wilton and York. Instruction to members for Weymouth and Appleby appeared in the *Flying Post* 20–23, 27–30 Dec 1701; and to those for Cornwall in Narcissus Luttrell, *A Brief Historical Relation of State Affairs* (1857) V 121.

57. Aylesbury, Wendover and Cambridge University in 1705, Buckinghamshire in 1708 and 1715, and London in 1715. Dr Lucy Sutherland informs me that the practice lapsed in the first half of the eighteenth century, so that the instructing which caused such controversy in Burke's day was a revival rather than a continuation of the techniques of Augustan politicians.

58. *A Collection of Addresses which have been presented to the Queen since the Impeachment of the Rev. Dr Henry Sacheverell* (1711).

59. Blenheim MSS B2–5: Somers to Marlborough, 14 [Apr] 1710.

60. Worcs RO, Pakington MSS: R. Prust to Lady Pakington, 30 June 1710.

61. BM Loan 29/321: newsletter, 5 Sep 1710.

62. [J. Oldmixon], *The History of Addresses*, 2nd ed. (1711) II 2.

63. Carlisle RO, Leconfield MS 169: W. Coles to J. Relfe, 18 Mar 1708.

64. Bodleian MS Top.Wilts. c7, folio 25.

65. Herefordshire RO, Bridges MSS: F. Bridges to W. Bridges, 23 Oct 1714.

CHAPTER THREE: PARTY ORGANISATION IN THE COUNTIES

1. Churchill College, Cambridge, Drax MSS: R. Walpole to Thomas Erle, 10 May 1708.

2. Christ Church Wake MSS, vol. XVII, folio 259: Nicolson to Wake, 7 Aug 1710.

3. HMC *Portland*, V 330–1: Lansdowne to Oxford, 11 Sep 1713.

4. BM Loan 29/147/2: duchess of Newcastle to Oxford, 13 Sep 1712.

5. HMC *Portland*, IV 153–4; for the Swarkeston Club in Derbyshire, the St Nicholas Club in Glamorganshire and the Cycle of the White Rose in Denbighshire and Flintshire see Geoffrey Holmes, *British Politics in the Age of Anne* (1967) p. 315.

6. Levens MSS: Bromley to Grahme, 13 Aug 1710.

7. Blenheim MSS D1–32: Wivel to Sunderland, 2 Aug 1707.

8. Walton Hall MSS, III 98.

9. NLW Bettisfield MS 32: Sir Thomas Hanmer to his cousin, 13 Nov 1714.

10. NLW Chirk Castle MS E1010: R. Wynne to Sir R. Myddleton, 13 Mar 1705; Leics RO, Finch MSS, box 4950, bdle 23: Sir R. Mostyn to Nottingham, 27 Apr 1708; NLW MS 1548F: Caernarvonshire agreement, 22 Apr 1708.

11. See Appendix C, p. 121.

12. Cornwall RO, Carew-Pole MS BO/23/63; HMC *Portland*, IV 607: J. Marley [*sic*: Manley] to Harley, 5 Oct 1710; BM Loan 29/302: A. Pendarves to Harley, 7 Oct 1710.

13. See Appendix A, pp. 115–17. The negotiations in Buckinghamshire before the 1715 election are very fully documented. See Huntington Library, Ellesmere MSS 10694–10771; Bodleian, Ballard MS 10, folios 29–30, 156–7; BM Loan 29/36/5 and 162/4.

14. John Rylands Library, Legh of Lyme MSS: J. Egerton to P. Legh, 12 Nov 1714.

15. For an example of an agreement in Cumberland see Bishop Nicolson's Diary, 31 Aug 1710, *Transactions of the Westmorland and Cumberland Antiquarian Society*, XXXCV 133–4.

16. Essex RO, MS DDL.C48: Lord Fitzwilliam to Dacre Barrett, 22 Dec 1704.

17. BM Loan 29/130/2: Cheyne to Harley, 22 Aug 1710.

18. Levens MSS: Carleton to Grahme, 18 Dec 1701.

19. Cambridge University Library, Cholmondley (Houghton) Corr. 405: J. Turner to Walpole, 19 Feb 1705; BM Add. MS 33084, folio 177: E. Townshend to Sir T. Pelham, 1 June 1705.

20. Carlisle RO, Lonsdale MSS: J. Lowther to W. Gilpin, 13 Apr 1707.

21. Northants RO, Isham Corr. 2745: Dolben to Isham, 21 Apr 1705.

22. Leeds RO, Temple Newsam MS 9/137: Somerset to Irwin, 13 Nov 1701.

23. Leics RO, Finch MSS, box 4969: Rutland poll 1713.

24. Northants RO, Isham Corr. 2736A: Dixon to Isham, 7 Feb 1705; ibid. 3712: Bertie to Isham, 16 May 1705.

25. BM Add. MS 35359, folio 14: H. Jacob to Philip Yorke, 21 Apr 1713.

26. *Wiltshire Archaeological and Natural History Magazine*, XLVI (1932) 80: H. Blake to W. White.

27. Worcs RO, Pakington MSS: Sir William Kent to Pakington, 28 Mar 1702.

28. 'The Note Book of Sir Walter Calverley, Bart', in *Surtees Society Publications*, LXXVII (1883) 119.

29. BM Stowe MS 748, folio 90.

30. Herefordshire RO, Bridges MSS: Scudamore to F. Bridges, 31 July 1713.

31. Cornwall RO, Carew-Pole MS BO/23/63: Granville to the sheriff of Cornwall, 29 Sept 1710: printed in *The Divided Society*, ed. Geoffrey Holmes and W. A. Speck (1967) p. 127.

32. HMC 10th Rep. App. part VI, *Dunster Castle* MSS, p. 81.

33. Leics Museum, Braye MS 3004.

34. Alnwick Castle MSS, vol. XXI i, folio 145: W. Walsh to the bishop of Oxford, 15 Apr 1702.

35. Levens MSS: Carleton to Grahme, 22 Jan 1708.

36. Carlisle RO, Lonsdale MSS: Lowther to Gilpin, 25 Nov 1707, 6 Jan 1708.

37. Huntington Library, Ellesmere MS 10713; Walton Hall MSS, III 46: printed in Elizabeth Hamilton, *The Mordaunts* (1966) p. 55.

38. Bodleian, Nicols Newspapers. For other examples see Mary Ransome, 'The Press in the Election of 1710', in *Cambridge Historical Journal*, VI (1939) 219–20.

39. HMC *Portland*, V 507–8: Lord Carlisle to anon., 20 Feb 1715.

40. Worcs RO, Pakington MSS: Thomas Gibson to Pakington, 17 Dec 1703; ibid. C. Stephens to Pakington, 5 Jan 1704; for a copy of Pakington's speech see W. Cobbett, *Parliamentary History* (1810) VI 153–5.

41. *A Letter to the Gentlemen and Freeholders of the County of Dorset concerning the next Election of Members of Parliament for the said County* (1713).

42. Carlisle RO, Lonsdale MSS, 'Parliamentary Elections, 1703, 1710'. The draft, dated 10 Dec 1701, ends 'this with a little alteration may serve for Westmorland'.

43. *Poems on Affairs of State* (1716) IV 4–5.

44. Leics Museum, Braye MSS 3022, 3023.

45. HMC *Portland*, IV 189: Dyer's newsletter, 29 May 1705.

46. e.g. Cambridgeshire, Norfolk and Yorkshire. BM Loan 29/321: Dyer's newsletter, 14, 24 Oct, 2 Nov 1710.

47. *Lincoln Record Society Publications*, vol. XLV: 'The Letters and Papers of the Banks Family of Revesby Abbey, 1704–1760', ed. J. W. F. Hill (Hereford, 1952) p. 13: the Rev. W. Steer to Joseph Banks, 23 Oct 1710.

48. *Grose's Classical Dictionary of the Vulgar Tongue*, ed. E. Partridge (1963) p. 263.

49. Berks RO, Trumbull MS liv: R. Bridges to Sir William Trumbull, 26 April 1710.

50. BM Add. MS 17677 HHH folio 449: L'Hermitage to the States-General, 2 Nov 1714.

51. HMC *Ailesbury*, p. 212: C. Beecher to Lord Bruce, 18 Sep 1713; *The Wentworth Papers*, ed. J. J. Cartwright (1883) p. 351: P. Wentworth to Lord Strafford, 8 Sep 1713.

52. Leics RO, Finch MSS, box 4969.

53. BM Add. MS 24612, folios 13–16; printed in *The Divided Society*, ed. Geoffrey Holmes and W. A. Speck (1967) pp. 158–60.

54. Walton Hall MSS, III 49; R. Burdet to Sir J. Mordaunt, 4 June 1705.

55. Blenheim MSS A2–38: Godolphin to Marlborough, 26 Apr 1708.

56. *Post Boy*, 7–10 Oct 1710.

57. Blenheim MSS D1–32: George Lucy to Sunderland, 17 Mar 1705.

58. Leics Museum, Braye MS 2863: Bretin to Cave, 12 Feb 1711.

59. See above, pp. 26–7.

60. Northants RO, Isham Corr. 2736B: T. Thornton to Isham, 27 Jan 1705.

61. BM Add. MS 33058, folio 225.

62. Leics Museum, Braye MS 2919: J. H. Cooper to Sir T. Cave, 9 Feb. 1715.

63. Bedford RO, MS W9.2653.

64. BM Add. MS 47026, p. 66: Parker to Sir John Perceval, 13 Oct 1710.

65. Longleat MSS, Thynne papers, XXVI, folio 116: Lord Stawell to Weymouth, 25 Mar 1711.

66. Huntington Library, Ellesmere MSS 10728–741; Nottingham University Library, Portland (Hollis) MS PW2.291a: Whichcote to Newcastle, 17 Oct 1710.

CHAPTER FOUR: PARTY ORGANISATION IN THE BOROUGHS

1. Bodleian, Willis MS 15, folio 126.

2. Sir Thomas Lawson-Tancred, *Records of a Yorkshire Manor* (1937) pp. 228–9.

3. Levens MSS: Carleton to Grahme, 29 Nov 1701.

4. Devon RO, Drake-King Corr. 346/F73.

5. Sir Thomas Lawson-Tancred, *Records of a Yorkshire Manor* (1937) pp. 231–2: Wenman to Wilkinson, 8 July 1711; ibid. pp. 241–2: Jessop to Wilkinson, 13 Jan 1713. For the attempts to buy up Sir Bryan Stapleton's estate see the correspondence of Thomas Pulleine in Nottingham University Library, Portland (Hollis) MS PW2.203–8.

6. See W. A. Speck, 'Conflict in Society', in *Britain after the Glorious Revolution*, ed. Geoffrey Holmes (1969), pp. 135–54.

7. Nottingham University Library, Portland (Hollis) MS PW2.208: R. Gowland to Pulleine, 23 Jan 1710.

8. *Verney Letters of the Eighteenth Century*, ed. Lady Verney (1930) I 301.

9. *The Diary of John Hervey, first Earl of Bristol* (Wells, 1894) passim; HMC 14th Report, VII *Records of the Corporation of Bury St Edmunds*, pp. 153–4.

10. *The Letter Books of John Hervey, first Earl of Bristol* (Wells, 1894) letter 289.

11. Cf. HMC *Portland*, IV 136: Defoe to Harley, 28 Sep 1704. 'Sir R. Davers, who rules this town . . .'

12. Though Hervey nominated to both seats after the by-election of Dec 1705, Davers tried to break this control as late as 1713. BM Loan 29/133/5: Davers to Oxford, 4 Mar 1714.

13. *Commons Journals*, XVI 419.

14. PRO 30/24/22/1/29: M. Ashley to Lord Shaftesbury, 2 Dec 1707.

15. Bishop Nicolson's Diary, 14 April 1708, in *Transactions of the Westmorland and Cumberland Antiquarian and Archaeological Society*, IV (1904) 30.

16. HMC *Portland*, V 229: Lansdowne to Oxford, 30 Sep 1712.

17. *Commons Journal*, XIV 49; BM Add. MS 27440, folio 136: Charles Allestree's memorandum book.

18. T. W. Whitley, *The Parliamentary Representation of the City of Coventry* (Coventry, 1894) pp. 139–40.

19. R. East, *Extracts from Records in the Possession of the Municipal Corporation of Portsmouth* (Portsmouth, 1891) p. 207.

20. For Brackley and Camelford see T. Carew, *An Historical Account of the Rights of Elections* (1755) I 69–71, 124–6; for Buckingham see 'The Case of the Borough of Buckingham', in *William Bromley's Parliamentary Papers* (Bodleian), IV 12; for Marlborough see HMC *Ailesbury*, pp. 216–24.

21. N. Luttrell, *A Brief Historical Relation of State Affairs* (1857) V 110–11.

22. Blenheim MSS D1–32: Lucy to Sunderland, 21 Feb 1705.

23. Corsham Court MSS: Somerset to Methuen, 7 Jan 1712.

24. HMC *Fortescue*, I 34: R. Pitt to T. Pitt, 3 Jan 1708.

25. Huntington Library, Stowe MS 58, III 99: W. Wotton to J. Brydges, 26 Oct 1708.

26. *A Collection of Several Paragraphs out of Mr Dyers's Letters* (1705) p. 1.

27. BM Burney Newspapers, *London Post*, 21 May 1705.

28. Geoffrey Holmes, *British Politics in the Age of Anne* (1967) pp. 318–23.

29. R. Walcott, 'The East India Interest in the General Election of 1700–1', in *English Historical Review*, LXXI (1956) 327–8.

30. *The Wentworth Papers*, ed. J. J. Cartwright (1883) p. 167: P. Wentworth to Lord Raby, 21 Dec 1710.

31. T. Carew, op. cit. I 137.

32. R. C. Gwilliam, 'The Chester Tanners and Parliament, 1711–1717', in *Chester Archaeological Society*, XCIV (1957) 41–9.

33. *Records of the Borough of Nottingham*, VI (Nottingham, 1914) 15.

34. Exeter City Library, City Archive, Ancient Letters, 464.

35. Christ Church Wake MSS, vol. XVII: Lloyd to Wake, 9 Oct 1710.

36. BM Loan 29/238 folio 364: Cowper to Newcastle, 27 Aug 1710.

37. HMC *Cowper*, II 451: Stanhope to Coke, 27 Jan 1702.

38. HMC *Dartmouth*, I 297: Blathwayt to Dartmouth, 14 Aug 1710.

39. HMC *Portland*, V 209: Bromley to Oxford, 30 July 1712.

40. Huntington Library, Stowe MS 57, III 166–7: Brydges to Captain Hereford, 3 Oct 1710.

41. HMC *Cowper*, II 421: P. Legh to Coke, 25 Feb 1701.

42. Corsham Court MSS: Somerset to Methuen, 7 Jan 1712.

43. Huntington Library, Stowe MS 57, II 29–30: Brydges to Godolphin, 31 Mar 1708.

44. *William Bromley's Parliamentary Papers* (Bodleian) II 119.

45. PRO 30/22/24/4, pp. 80–2: Shaftesbury to Somers, 13 May 1708.

46. Bridport, Knaresborough and Scarborough.

47. Carlisle RO, Leconfield MS 169: J. Relfe to anon., 4 Mar 1708.

48. Carlisle RO, Carleton MSS: T. Carleton to T. Lutwyche, 6 June 1713.

49. *Commons Journals*, XV 38.

50. Leics RO, Finch MSS, box 4969: Chetwynd to Lord Finch, 13 Jan 1715.

51. Herefordshire RO, Bridges MSS: F. Bridges to W. Bridges, 4, 25 Sep 1714.

52. Carlisle RO, Leconfield MS 110.

53. T. Carew, op. cit. passim.

54. Ibid. I 66; II 132.

55. Leics RO, Finch MSS, box 4969: J. Chetwynd to Lord Finch, 14 Feb 1715; BM Add. MS 33060, folio 18.

56. Dorset RO, Fox-Strangways MSS; HMC *Ailesbury*, p. 204: C. Beecher to Lord Bruce, 10 July 1711.

57. Levens MSS: Carleton to Grahme, 21 Nov 1702.

58. Berks RO, Neville MS D/EN.F23/2.

59. Carlisle RO, Leconfield MS 110.

60. Carew, op. cit. II 145.

61. Bodleian, Ballard MS 21, folio 222: J. Baron to [Dr Charlett], 23 May [1705].

62. BM Loan 29/321: Dyer's newsletter, 7 Nov 1710.

63. e.g. Southwark, King's Lynn, Minehead and Hindon. *Flying Post*, 22–25 Aug, 1–3, 8–10, 12 Sep 1713.

64. *Blundell's Diary*, ed. T. E. Gibson (Liverpool, 1895) p. 117.

65. *Flying Post*, 5–7 June 1705.

66. Bodleian, Rawlinson MSS, Letter 40, folio 63: anon. to J. Barnes, n.d.

67. *A Collection of Several Paragraphs out of Mr Dyers's Letters* (1705) p. 4.

68. Leics RO, Finch MSS, box 4969: Chetwynd to Lord Finch, 13 Jan 1715.

69. Huntington Library, Stowe MS 57, XI 90: Brydges to Philpotts, 1 Nov 1714.

70. Ibid. 58, X 168: Woodhouse to Brydges, 20 Feb 1712.

71. Surrey RO, W. Bryant, 'List and State of Reigate Burgages'.

### CHAPTER FIVE: THE SAFE SEATS

1. See Appendix C, pp. 121–2.

2. Geoffrey Holmes, 'The Influence of the Peerage in English Parliamentary Elections, 1702–1713' (unpublished B. Litt. thesis, Oxford, 1951) p. 50.

3. Ibid. pp. 191, 194.

4. Christ Church Wake MSS, vol. XVII misc. i, letter 243: W. Wotton to Bishop Wake, 21 Mar 1710.

5. Anon., *A Vindication of the Last Parliament in Four Dialogues between Sir Simon and Sir Peter* (1711) pp. 151, 152.

6. G. Davies, 'The Election at Hereford in 1702', in *Huntington Library Quarterly*, XII (1948–9) 325–6.

7. Huntington Library, Stowe MS 57, III 166–7: Brydges to Captain Hereford, 3 Oct 1710. See above, p. 57.

8. Ibid. II 28: Brydges to Marlborough, 13 Apr 1708.

9. Cambridge University Library, Cholmondley (Houghton) Corr. 216: J. Turner to R. Walpole, 8 May 1702.

10. Northumberland RO, Blackett MS ZBL.18Q: Newby Hall Letterbook, 14 Sep [1710].

11. Bodleian, Willis MS 15, folio 6.

12. R. Walcott, *English Politics in the Early Eighteenth Century* (1956) pp. 200–15.

13. [R. Steele], *Memoirs of the Life of the Most Noble Thomas, late Marquess of Wharton* (1715) p. 41.

14. J. Carswell, *The Old Cause* (1954) p. 74.

15. Sir Thomas Lee at Aylesbury, Fleetwood Dormer at Wycomb, Wharton Dunch at Appleby, and John Hutton at Richmond.

16. Thomas Lamplugh was an odd political bird. He was an occasional conformist (Kendal RO, Hothfield MSS: T. Carleton to Lord Thanet, 2 Aug 1702). He was also a Whig who voted on the Court side. This led me to assume that he was returned on the duke of Somerset's interest when I wrote 'The Choice of a Speaker in 1705', in *Bulletin of the Institute of Historical Research*, XXXVII (1964) 34, n 2. But it is clear from the poll-books at Cockermouth castle that he stood against the interests of both Somerset and Wharton in 1702 and 1705. Carlisle RO, Leconfield MS 107.

17. Sir Lewis Namier, *The Structure of Politics at the Accession of George III* (1957) p. 150.

18. HMC *Portland*, IV 551: Weymouth to Harley, 24 July 1710.

19. BM Add. MS 29588, folios 93–4 Winchilsea to Nottingham, 12 July 1702.

20. BM Add. MS 34223, folio 15.

21. BM Add. MS 28887, folio 374: J. Macky to J. Ellis, 16 Nov 1701.

22. BM Add. MS 33512; Kent RO, MS Sa/ZB2.

23. Kent RO, MSS Sa/ZB2/154 156: letters to Sandwich Corporation from S. Masham and R. Bowles, 5 Oct 1702, and J. Mitchel, 20 Nov 1702.

24. Walcott, op. cit. pp. 36–9 and app. II; cf. Geoffrey Holmes, *British Politics in the Age of Anne* (1967) pp. 362–4.

25. Holmes, op. cit. p. 364.

26. Huntington Library, Stowe MS 57, II 29–30: Brydges to Godolphin, 31 Mar 1708.

27. Holmes, op. cit. p. 258.

28. Blenheim MSS A1–20: St John to Marlborough, 25 May 1705.

CHAPTER SIX: THE FLOATING VOTE

1. BM Loan 29/160/2: H. Walpole to Harley, n.d.; cf. above, p. 34.

2. Geoffrey Holmes, *British Politics in the Age of Anne* (1967) p. 19.

3. BM Loan 29/321: Dyer's newsletter, 9 May 1710.

4. *London Post*, 14 May 1705.

5. BM Add. MS 5833, folio 107: Henry Crossgrove to John Strype, Norwich, 2 Dec 1714.

6. Bucks RO, Claydon House Letters, reel 51: 'Copy of my letter to Wm Lord Viscount Cheyne', 19 Dec 1700.

7. Carlisle RO, Lonsdale MSS: James Lowther to William Gilpin, 2 Sep 1710.

8. Lord Campbell, *Lives of the Lord Chancellors* (1846) IV 428.

9. Blenheim MSS D1–21: Wharton to Sunderland, 20 Apr 1708.

10. *William Bromley's Parliamentary Papers* (Bodleian) I 72; BM Loan 29/10/22 and 25. For the whole episode see P. Styles, 'The Corporation of Bewdley under the later Stuarts', in *University of Birmingham Historical Journal*, I (1947–8) 92–133.

11. Blenheim MSS D1–32: Holland to Sunderland, 11 Aug 1707.

12. Hertfordshire RO, Panshanger MSS: Sharp to Cowper, 21 July 1707.

13. Lord Campbell, *Lives of the Lord Chancellors*, IV (1846) 429.

14. *The Divided Society*, ed. Geoffrey Holmes and W. A. Speck (1967) p. 46.

15. BM Loan 29/191, folio 276: R. Duke to Harley, 20 Sep 1704.

16. John Rylands Library, Legh of Lyme Muniments: J. Ward to P. Legh, 21 Mar 1704.

17. Blenheim MSS D2–2: Fleming to Sunderland, 29 Apr 1704 (copy in Bodleian, Carte MS 109, folios 67–8); BM Loan 29/9/5: Cabinet Minutes, 16 July 1704.

18. William Salt Library, Dartmouth MS D1778 (v) 779: Finch to Dartmouth, n.d.

19. BM Loan 29/27/19.

20. Essex RO, DDKw.01/37/1.

21. BM Loan 29/156/12: Beaufort to Oxford, 6 Sep 1713.

22. Northants RO, Isham Corr. 1804: Sir J. Isham to J. Isham, 20 Sep 1714.

23. Worcs RO, Pakington MSS: S. Pytts to Lady Pakington, 4 May 1705.

24. Levens MSS: Lawson to Grahme, 9 May 1705. When James Lowther began to make interest in Cumberland in 1707 he wrote to his agent, 'my cousin . . . being sheriff I suppose I may make sure of having the election at the most convenient place for me'. Carlisle RO, Lonsdale MSS: Lowther to Gilpin, 25 Nov 1707. Later, in 1711, the place of election in Cumberland was fixed by statute.

25. BM Loan 29/321: newsletter, 4 Nov 1710.

26. Essex RO, DDKw.02.

27. PRO 30/24/22/2: Shaftesbury to Cowper, 2 Dec 1705; BM Loan 29/130/2: Cheyne to Oxford, 12 Nov 1713.

28. *The Wentworth Papers*, ed. J. J. Cartwright (1883) p. 135: P. Wentworth to Lord Raby, 18 Aug 1710.

29. T. Forster, *Original Letters of Locke, Algernon Sidney and Lord Shaftesbury* (1830) pp. 179–80: Shaftesbury to Furly, 10 Aug 1702.

30. HMC *Cowper*, III 13: J. Bromley to T. Coke, 20 July 1702.

31. Onno Klopp, *Der Fall des Hauses Stuart* (Vienna, 1887) XIV 675: Robethon to the elector of Hanover, 21 Mar 1711.

32. *Miscellaneous State Papers . . . of the Earl of Hardwicke*, ed. Philip Yorke (1778) II 453.

33. *The Letters of Joseph Addison*, ed. J. Graham (1941) p. 110: Addison to Manchester, 20 Apr 1708.

34. *Private Correspondence of Sarah, Duchess of Marlborough* (1838) I 318: Craggs to the duchess, 18 May 1710.

35. *Commons Journals*, XIII 644.

36. *Instructions to Freeholders drawn from Her Majesty's Most Gracious Speech from the Throne on Thursday the 16th of July 1713 to both Houses of Parliament* (1713).

37. *Commons Journals*, XVIII 14; reprinted in *English Historical Documents*, ed. D. C. Douglas, vol. X *1714–1783*, ed. D. B. Horn and Mary Ransome (1957) p. 149.

38. N. C. Hunt, *Two Early Political Associations* (Oxford, 1961) pp. 1–52, 113–29.

39. *A Collection of Several Paragraphs out of Mr Dyer's's Letters* (1705) p. 4.

40. *Commons Journals*, XVI 57.

41. BM Loan 29/320: Dyer's newsletter, 25 Jan 1709.

42. HMC *Portland*, II 222: Heathcote to Newcastle, 30 Sep 1710.

43. *The Divided Society*, ed. Geoffrey Holmes and W. A. Speck (1967) p. 57.

44. *Observator*, 28 Apr–2 May 1705.

45. BM Add. MS 29579, folio 394: Sir Charles Lyttleton to Lord Hatton, 8 July 1702.

46. Ibid. folios 396, 401: same to same, 10, 15 July 1702.

47. BM Add. MS 27440, folio 134.

48. HMC *Portland*, IV 214: Defoe to Harley, 30 July 1705.

49. Ibid. 641: J. Durden to Harley, 5 Dec 1710.

50. BM Add. MS 17677CCC, folio 443: L'Hermitage to the States-General, 27 April 1708.

51. *Remarks and Collections of Thomas Hearne*, ed. H. E. Salter (Oxford, 1897) IV 227.

52. T. Carew, *An Historical Account of the Rights of Elections* (1755) I 188.
53. See above, pp. 61–2.
54. Carlisle RO, Lonsdale MSS: Henry Newman to James Lowther, 6 Aug 1713.
55. The stamp duty of 1712 cut this total down to the mid-reign figure. See J. R. Sutherland 'The Circulation of Newspapers and Literary Periodicals 1700–30', in *Library*, XV (1935) 110, 111; J. M. Price, 'A Note on the Circulation of the London Press, 1704–1714', in *Bulletin of the Institute of Historical Research*, XXXI (1958) 215–24.
56. BM Loan 29/130/4: J. Clare to Harley, report on the Press 1705.
57. *A Collection of Several Paragraphs out of Mr Dyer's Letters* (1705); partly printed in HMC *Portland*, IV 188–90.
58. BM Add. MS 28893, folio 137: W. Bowes to J. Ellis, 18 May 1705.
59. 'The Freeholders', no. 22, printed in *Select Documents for Queen Anne's Reign*, ed. G. M. Trevelyan (1929) p. 71.
60. There is a small selection in *Political Ballads*, ed. W. Walker Wilkins (1860) vol. II.
61. A. Boyer, *The Political State of Great Britain* (1718) I 18. Harley described the City election of 1705 as being of 'great consequence to give life to others'. BM Loan 29/9/12: list of constituencies, 7 Feb 1705.
62. J. Loftis, *The Politics of Drama in Augustan England* (Oxford, 1963).
63. R. J. Allan, 'The Kit-Cat Club and the Theatre', in *Review of English Studies*, VII (1931) 56–61.
64. *Spence's Anecdotes*, ed. J. Underhill (1890) p. 110.
65. O. W. Furly, 'The Pope-burning Processions of the Late Seventeenth Century', in *History*, XLIV (1959) 16–23.
66. J. Swift, *Journal to Stella*, ed. Temple Scott (1897) p. 283.
67. Lincs RO, Massingberd Corr. 20/89: Burrell Massingberd to Sir William Massingberd, 28 Feb 1710.
68. G. Burnet, *History of My Own Time* (Oxford, 1833) V 444–5.
69. A. Boyer, *The History of the Reign of Queen Anne digested into Annals* (1710) IX 202.
70. HMC *Portland*, IV 550: T. Foley to Harley, 17 June 1710.
71. *Examiner*, no. 28.
72. HMC *Cowper*, III 29–30: M. Burton to T. Coke; Coke's suspect church-manship eroded and by 1710 destroyed his interest in Derbyshire. Ibid. p. 84: Elizabeth Coke to same, 3 June 1710; HMC *Portland*, IV 612: Coke to Harley, 11 Oct 1710.
73. Lincs RO, Monson MS 7/13/124: Gervase Scrope to Sir J. Newton, 1 July 1710.
74. Bodleian, Ballard MS 15, folio 96: J. Johnson to Dr Charlett, 15 Sep 1710.
75. BM Add. MS 24612, folio 14.
76. Blenheim MS E36: Halifax to the duchess of Marlborough, 15 May 1705.
77. Ibid.
78. Bodleian MSS, Film 297: newsletter, 10 May 1705.
79. HMC *Portland*, IV 180: St John to Harley, 15 May 1705.
80. *Calendar of State Papers Domestic 1700–1702*, p. 452: newsletter.
81. E. N. Williams, *The Eighteenth Century Constitution* (Cambridge, 1960) p. 138.

82. Anon., *Occasional Thoughts concerning our Present Divisions and their Remedies* (1704) pp. 10–11.

## CHAPTER SEVEN: THE GENERAL ELECTION OF 1705

1. *Poems on Affairs of State* (1716) IV 4–5, 109.
2. BM Add. MS 17677 AAA, folios 213, 271: L'Hermitage to the States-General, 30 March, 4 May 1705.
3. John Comyns and Henry Lloyd: see HMC *Bath*, I 69: Godolphin to Harley, 2 May 1705; BM Loan 29/263 p. 75: Harley to Lord Keeper, 2 May 1705.
4. *London Gazette*, 19–23 Apr 1705.
5. BM Loan 29/9/12: list dated 7 Feb 1705.
6. For Dyer's newsletters see *A Collection of Several Paragraphs out of Mr Dyers's newsletters* (1705).
7. Letters from Halifax to the duchess of Marlborough of [10,] 12, 15 and 22 May 1705 are in Blenheim MS E36.
8. BM Burney newspapers.
9. For a list of Tackers see my Oxford D.Phil. thesis 'The House of Commons 1702–1714: a study in political organisation', pp. 102–8.
10. Bodleian, Carte MS 244, folios 58–9: Thomas Carte to his father, 19 May 1705; Bodleian MSS, Film 297: newsletter, 15 May 1705; Bodleian, Rawlinson MS A245, folio 71: commonplace book of Anthony Hammond, 26 Mar 1705.
11. Bodleian, Willis MS 9, folio 148.
12. Blenheim MS E20: Godolphin to the duchess of Marlborough, 'Friday at 7'.
13. For developments between the election and the session see my thesis, 'The House of Commons 1702–14', pp. 141–50.
14. Nottingham University Library, Portland MS PWa.410: 'Mr. Eyles' to Lord Portland, 25 July 1705.
15. Sir Winston Churchill, *Marlborough, his Life and Times* (1936) III 24: Marlborough to Godolphin, 25 June 1705.

## CHAPTER EIGHT: CONCLUSION: ELECTION RESULTS 1701–15

1. BM Add. MS 30000E, folio 420: Bonet to Frederick III, 16 Dec 1701; translated in *The Divided Society*, ed. Geoffrey Holmes and W. A. Speck (1967) p. 19.
2. G. Burnet, *History of My Own Time* (Oxford, 1833) V 45.
3. BM Add. MS 9102, folio 8: Hamilton to Sunderland, 1 June 1708.
4. Bodleian, Carte MS 244, folio 127: Wood to Carte, 18 Nov 1710.
5. BM Stowe MS 225, folio 208; Schutz to Robethon, 29 Sep 1713; translated in *The Divided Society*, ed. Holmes and Speck, p. 32.
6. Ibid. p. 32; Huntington Library, Loudun MS LO10924: Cathcart to Loudun, 18 Feb 1715.
7. Cf. G. M. Trevelyan, *England under Queen Anne* (1932) II 350; J. H. Plumb, *Sir Robert Walpole* (1956) I 142.
8. Cf. K. Feiling, *History of the Tory Party* (1924) p. 423; G. M. Trevelyan, *England under Queen Anne* (1934) III 348, n 78.

9. R. Walcott, *English Politics in the Early Eighteenth Century* (Oxford, 1956) passim.

10. Ibid. p. 34.

11. The evidence on which this paragraph is based is discussed in my Oxford D.Phil. thesis 'The House of Commons 1702–1714: a study in political organisation', pp. 59–101.

12. See Appendix D, p. 121.

13. BM Add. MS 22851, folio 121: Craggs to Pitt, 25 Feb 1702.

14. *Letters and Correspondence* . . . *of the Right Honourable Henry St John, Lord Viscount Bolingbroke*, ed. G. Parke (1798) I 11: St John to Drummond, 10 Nov 1710.

# Index